Because peo

building an economy th.

Jurriaan Kamp

PARAVIEW
Special Editions

New York

Because People Matter
Copyright © 2003 Jurriaan Kamp
All rights reserved. No part of this book may be used or reproduced
in any manner whatsoever without prior written permission except
in the case of brief quotations embodied in critical articles or
reviews. For information address Paraview Special Editions,
P.O. Box 416, Old Chelsea Station, New York, NY 10113-0416,
or visit our website at www.paraview.com.

Cover illustration: Hans Kennis
Book design: Pieter Kers.

ISBN: 1-931044-45-7

Library of Congress Catalog Number: 2002116483

CONTENTS

For Hélène, Devika, Majlie, Nina and Wali
because they matter the most

After all, human beings weren't created just to keep the economy going.
    – Loesje

INTRODUCTION: WARNING

The Indian novelist Arundhati Roy recently wrote an essay on the gigantic complex of dams in the Narmada Valley in India. Her story illustrates with painful precision the degrading way our modern world economy works. The Narmada project has already made millions of people homeless. Reservoirs have caused the disappearance of agricultural lands, and cattle have drowned. Soon another dam is to be completed and another two hundred thousand Indians will be driven away. Filled with outrage, Roy writes, "The mere participation in a debate over housing signifies a first step towards the suspension of every principle of justice. The forced relocation of two hundred thousand people in order to provide drinking water for forty million, or even entertaining the pretension that such a thing is possible – there's something totally wrong with the scale at which this work is being undertaken. This is the mathematics of fascism. It causes stories to be strangled and details to be clubbed to death, and perfectly reasonable people become blinded by a misleading but brilliant vision."

Typical India. It seems so far away, like a story about another world where, unfortunately, other norms apply. But that's not what this is. I have become aware that the same "mathematics" is plaguing our own society. We're now in the midst of economic prosperity and fewer factories are being closed. But how long ago was it when thousands of people lost their jobs because of mergers or shutdowns? Granted, those people were not sent to their deaths, as the Indian country dwellers are; they're given a tidy sum of unemployment payments by way of the social security system. Yet the idea behind the calculation is the same: the worldwide domination of big money. In either case, the interests of the individual are not primary. The modern economy is far more likely to be based on the dutch "postergirl" Loesje's ironic comment.

How could human beings have created a system of trade and production in which human beings don't matter? That's the wrong question, many will hasten to respond. Free trade and the market economy are bringing prosperity to the farthest corners of the planet today. Prosperity in figures, yes. But if all those factors are added up – factors that are not expressed in figures and that are precisely the ones having to do with this human quality of life – there would be little or nothing left over from all this improvement. The economy serves the gross national product, the stock market and the shareholders. Behind all those institutes are human beings, of course, but their voices don't count.

Take the mantra of bigness. Business are becoming bigger and bigger because the globalization of the world economy demands it, because "bigger" is the same as "better." That's why your bank has changed names three times in the past ten years. That's why airline companies have to merge just to "survive." That's why "the biggest merger ever" has become the monthly refrain of the financial pages. These kinds of mergers may be in the interest of the shareholders, but they are not in the interest of people. Boards of directors can come up with very fancy calculations regarding scale advantages, but those calculations mention nothing about the frustrations that more and more employees are experiencing within these ever-expanding organizations. There's little different between these calculations and Arundhati Roy's "mathematics of fascism."

It's a peculiar world where fathers – still almost always *fathers* – deal with their companies as they would never deal with their own families, and treat the earth as they would never treat their own back yards. It's a peculiar world where housekeeping – that's the definition of the word "economy" – means something entirely different at the national level than it does at the level of the individual home. It's a peculiar world when we keep telling ourselves that all those abuses – human rights violations, environmental pollution, child labor, stress – are just unavoidable consequences of "progress," as if inhumanity were a condition for humanity.

Those multinational companies and international organizations, such as the World Bank, the International Monetary Fund (IMF) and the World Trade Organization (WTO), don't just do whatever they like. They operate according to rules and principles that are consciously made and chosen. Free trade, gross national product, interest, debts, growth, productivity, efficiency – all these concepts are formulated with care. The gathering of heads of state and governmental leaders at Bretton Woods in the United States in 1944, for instance – when the IMF and the World Bank were created – determined to a great extent how the world economy would develop up to the present day. This is often forgotten. We are not condemned to the present state of affairs; it is something we – or at least those whom we have appointed for this task – have chosen.

And that is why we can choose to take a new path. Agreements were made in the past, so there's no reason why we can't make new ones today – new agreements with new, different, consequences, agreements that might bring about a new economy. I'm not talking about the new internet economy. The digital economy isn't based on anything new, nor does it regard the human individual as central. No, the search for an essentially new economy is still going on, and it's been progressing well. In the past five years, many interesting books have been published by authors who have carefully analyzed the shortcomings of current economic thought and procedures, and who are presenting new, pioneering visions of economic development. But it isn't only new ideas that are on the horizon. What is most promising is that those ideas are striking sympathetic chords in wider and wider circles. The mass protest during the meeting of the World Trade Organization in Seattle in November 1999 was illustrative. The demonstrators who went to Seattle were not mainly the well-known "professional" activists from organizations such as Greenpeace. There were priests, teachers, students, writers and especially fathers and grandfathers, mothers and grandmothers: ordinary people who threw themselves into the breach for an economy that has room for their values, ideals and longings.

In September 2000, the *State of the World Forum* was held in New York, always a fascinating encounter between the established order and representatives of the new way of thinking. And once again, the focus was on globalization. As it turned out, the established order had already been contaminated with the "Seattle virus." Whether it was the Thai minister of foreign affairs or the leading partner of the McKinsey consultancy, criticism came from unexpected corners of the galloping liberalization of world trade, in which fundamental human values are being irretrievably swept away. These kinds of opinions and analyses are forming the basis of the policy reform to come.

This book presents a number of ideas intended to support and further stimulate the development of a number of ideas. The book is not exhaustive. There is so much more that is leading in the right direction. But I have chosen a number of fundamental concepts which, when provided with new substance, could become the basis for new agreements for organizing the world economy. The ideas are the products of many brains. A few authors and institutes have been particularly inspiring to me. The work *Redefining Progress* breaks entirely new ground when it comes to calculating gross national product (see chapter 1). The new book by the Belgian banker Bernard Lietaer, *The Future of Money*, is an important contribution on the way to a humane economy (see chapter 2). With his horrifying analysis in *The Grip of Death*, the British author and teacher Michael Rowbotham opened my eyes to the fact that our whole economy runs on debts. And in his essay on Seattle, Paul Hawken showed me that you can be on the side of trade without having to support current international trade policy. The book ends with the ideas of the man who inspired its title, E.F. Schumacher. His *Small is Beautiful* could still serve as a bible for world economic reform.

The book is organized in two parts. The first part (chapters 1, 2, 3, 4, 5, and 6) deals with the economy at large – trade, countries and businesses. We have influence on that economy – indirect influence perhaps, but remember the former Prime Minister who called on people to show their anger. The second part (chapters 7, 8 and 9) deals with the small-scale economy of home and the workplace: how we ourselves decide how we work and how we consume resources, and what kind of growth we are aiming for in our lives. For if the focus in our daily lives is on human beings – our neighbors – this choice will ultimately reach the economy at large. It's simple: if we want people to matter, then they matter. It begins with a choice, for you and for me.

This choice brings me back to the outrage expressed by Arundhati Roy and the former Prime Minister of a leading Western European country, who pounded his fist on the table at the State of the World Forum in New York and said, "We must show our anger. Only when we show our anger will governments change their policy." He should know. But in order to get angry we have to know what we're talking about. We have to know what's going on in order to feel involved. You have to know what's going on to realize that you yourself are contributing to developments that you have carefully considered and regard with abhorrence. This is what happens to me when I read the story about the dams in India. I can no longer deny it; I take it personally. I, too, allow the World Bank to do whatever it pleases, carrying out its pernicious policy in developing countries. I, too, buy products from multinational corporations that violate human rights, or from companies that do less than they could to make their production sustainable.

I also accept that 200 of the biggest companies in the world together own more then 80% of the world population. Outrageous enrichment goes hand in hand with incredible pauperisation. What is the similarity between Zambia and the investment-bank Goldman Sachx, The Guardian recently asked? The answer illustrates the madness of the world economy. Zambia earns 2.2 billion dollars per year for its 25 million inhabitants. Goldman Sachs earns per year 2.6 billion dollars for its 161 partners.

As soon as you know what sort of damage is being inflicted by the globalization of the world economy as it is now developing, you can no longer deny your own complicity. As soon as you know that there are alternatives, you find yourself challenged to summon the courage to strive for renewal. That is why I am writing this book – as the bearer of both bad tidings and good. You have been warned.

Rotterdam, November 2000
Jurriaan Kamp

GNP measures neither our wit nor our courage, neither our wisdom nor our learning, neither our compassion nor our devotion to our country. It measures everything, in short, except that which makes life worthwhile.

– Robert Kennedy

I GROWTH. WHAT GROWTH?

The most sacred foundation of the current economic order is "growth." Anyone who dares raise questions about economic growth is immediately branded a heretic. To begin with, let's get one thing straight: I do not think that a human being or a society can live without growth. On the contrary, growth is inherent in life itself. But growth has many guises in any human life. A child needs new shoes every year. In an adult's life, it's insight and experience that grow. There is an entire dimension of spiritual growth (see chapter 9) that is vital for the future of humanity but cannot be captured in statistics. In the ordinary human life, "more" is not always "better." Someone who weighs a hundred kilos is not better off if he weighs two hundred. Not every rising chart reflects progress. If it has to do with the economy, however, there is no distinction; all growth is good news. But this vision is now being recognized as a myth, as a way of thinking in which the human individual is ultimately no longer the focus of the economy.

First of all, when the headlines start crowing that economic growth for the second quarter was higher than expected, let's examine *what* it is that's growing. That growth has to do with the increase in the gross national product (GNP). The GNP consists of the sum of what all the inhabitants of a country earn. To be more exact, the GNP is the combined value of all a country's products and services. The idea is that as the GNP rises, the prosperity of the country increases. Recent research by the World Bank underscores this principle. The report "Growth is Good for the

Poor" demonstrates that as the GNP of a country rises, the incomes of all the inhabitants of that country – taken on the average – show the same increase. This is how the economists of the World Bank counter the familiar criticism that economic growth mostly benefits the rich. The report concludes enthusiastically that the globalization of the world economy leads to higher incomes, and that the poor profit as much as the rich do. So economic growth is good, you might say.

Yet it's not so simple. It seems that the rise of incomes within an economy has little to do with the health of the economy. William Easterly, another economist from the World Bank, did a study of 95 parameters to determine to what extent economic growth had also led to increased prosperity. His study covered the period 1960-2000. Easterly found only five indicators that had improved: the number of telephones in a country, the number of commercial vehicles and the intake of calories and proteins, and there seemed to be a connection between economic growth and governments breaking fewer of their contracts. That was all. Easterly was rather bewildered by the results and ended the official World Bank study with the words, "The evidence that life gets better during growth is surprisingly uneven."

So whereas economic growth does result in higher incomes – more money – it does not result in prosperity. The Irish economist and journalist Richard Douthwaite comes to the same conclusion in his book *The Growth Illusion.* He studied the period 1955-1988 in Great Britain. During that period, the British GNP doubled. But at the same time there was evidence of a rise in criminality, the number of divorces and suicides, the rate of absenteeism at work and the number of chronic illnesses. In other words, material progress did not bring happiness to the British. Economic growth has proven itself an inefficient instrument in the pursuit of social improvement, and the gross national product is not a particularly relevant gauge.

There are countries with a low GNP where the prosperity of the population is visibly higher than countries with a higher GNP. A favorite example concerns the Indian state of Kerala. The national per capita income for the population of Kerala is 1/70th of the Western level. But the life expectation of the average West European man is 73; in Kerala it is 70 years of age. Illiteracy has been completely eliminated in Kerala, and the birth rate fluctuates around eighteen per thousand, as opposed to sixteen in the Netherlands, for example. Development experts work with something called a "Physical Quality of Life Index," which provides a number between 1 and 100 for the most important indicators for the quality of human life. Kerala scores 88 on this scale, far beyond the levels of the developing countries of Africa and Asia and close to the level of the rich West. Health and education are at the same level as the West – and this is without money. And it's also without a growing economy, since the economy of Kerala, according to the usual criteria, has been characterized by stagnation for many years now.

The same phenomenon can be seen even closer to home. Resear-chers also discovered that the quality of life in Ireland – before the country had opened its borders to European integration – was strikingly high in comparison with the level of its GNP. The Irish were considerably less "rich" than the British, but the quality of their lives was not lower. This mystery is explained by the curious way the GNP is calculated. The more self-supporting a country is, the lower the GNP. But the man who picks apples from his own tree is not less happy than the man who buys apples from the supermarket. Quite possibly just the opposite is true. And the same holds for the man who builds his own house. Therein lies the secret of the Irish and the people of Kerala.

The problem with the gross national product is that it makes no distinctions; all activities are added together. The GNP works like a calculator that can add but cannot subtract. It does not discriminate between costs and assets, or between productive and destructive activities. Everything that takes place in the market is regarded as profit for humanity. At the same time, everything that cannot be expressed in terms of money is ignored – regardless of its importance for the common good. Thus the family, the community and nature play no role in the GNP, but the quality of those elements determines how we experience life to a significant degree.

The family and a commercial enterprise know the difference between costs and assets. At home, the expenses for medical care and housing are subtracted from the earned income. In the GNP, conversely, costs and assets are added together. If a factory sells its machines – its capital – this may very well result in income, but it also results in a downswing in the balance sheet. Consequently, the gross national product of Brazil is skyrocketing while the entire Amazon rain forest is being cut down. Even worse: if the Brazilians grind all those trees into wood chips and go to the casino with the proceeds, they become richer – according to the GNP. If herring as a species is threatened by intensive fishing, this is regarded as a source of income by the national accounting department. If crime in a country increases and more money is spent fighting it, the economy receives an impulse. The more lawyers put to work on the growing number of divorces, the higher the GNP. An earthquake or a devastating hurricane is a blessing for the economy. Environmental pollution counts double. If a chemical company makes a product that pollutes, that counts; and if that product later ends up in the wrong place and the government has to dig up the polluted land, it counts once more. You can go on and on. This form of national bookkeeping creates the impression that a safe society and the protection of natural resources and the environment are being sacrificed for the sake of the economy. Economic growth can go hand in hand with social decay – but you would never know from the gross national product.

There are important activities that are not included, either. If a mother lovingly cares for her children, the economy stagnates. If she reads them a story, nothing happens. But if parents take their children to a daycare center or let them watch television, the gross national product goes up. All the work carried on by volunteers, without which the world of sports, for example, would come to a standstill, does not count. It's not good for the economy if children care for their aged parents. A nursing home, on the other hand, contributes to "progress." And then there's the remarkable consumption game: those who eat too much, and are thereby included in the count, grow overweight. We then spend millions more on weight-loss products to lose all that extra weight – that counts, too. The bypass patient is a metaphor for a nation's progress: develop unhealthy eating habits, pay for the consequences, add this up and the economy has grown a bit more.

The fascinating thing is that the man who devised this system was quick to raise his own objections to it. In 1932, a young American economist, Simon Kuznets, was put to work drawing up criteria for the national accounting department. The depression was over; it was the time of Keynes's reparable economy. Politics needed instruments, and a gross national product was such an instrument. But even in his first report to the American Congress in 1934, Kuznets warned of the limitations of the new system. Later he wrote, "Goals for 'more' growth should specify more growth of what and for what." But this important comment was lost. The politicians went wild with their crippled calculator so they could impress the emperor. It's like playing a game with a pair of dice that always land on the same number.

So the gross national product says little about the actual prosperity in a country, as the examples of Ireland and Kerala demonstrate. Many different progressive economists have tried to come up with better methods for calculating national income. In these alternative methods, activities such as housework and voluntary work *are* included. Money that is spent fighting crime or repairing the damage caused by crime, however, is subtracted from the national income. Hospital bills or the invoice that the carpenter sends for repairing a jimmied door are posted as negative entries. Expenses involved in cleaning up pollution are also subtracted. And a country that consumes its oil or gas reserves must enter that consumption in the books as expenses.

Using these methods, these same economists then began recalculating economic growth since World War Two. And what did they find? According to these various methods of calculation, there has been absolutely no indication of progress since 1970. The quality of life is not improving, despite the fact that according to the customary norms the GNP in those countries has doubled since 1970 – with one exception: Germany. According to the new methods there is evidence of growth there since reunification took place. And this is understandable, since investments in the infrastructure of the former DDR are clearly contributing to the improvement of living conditions in that part of Germany.

The tragic conclusion is that since 1970, economic growth in the West has been futile. There was more money, but it did not result in better quality of life. There were more cars, but there were also more traffic jams and exhaust gasses. And the higher salaries were accompanied by more stress and less time. The recalculation of the national incomes is in keeping with most people's experience. Who can really say that the quality of their life has doubled in the past thirty years? The introduction of a new method of calculating the national income – with costs and assets, adding and subtracting – would bring economic development closer to human experience. A realistic national income would make an important contribution to an economy in which people count, because such a national income places a value on *all* work and the *entire* environment.

The futile development of the economy since 1970 is even more distressing when you realize that the national debt in most countries has mushroomed in the intervening years. The Dutch national debt grew from 50 to 500 billion guilders between 1970 and 2000. This rising debt is used to finance economic growth. But debts have to be paid – with interest. You can pay that interest from your current budget at the cost of other expenses, but nobody wants to do that. Or you can pay the interest with the profits you earn from new activities. Those profits require more growth. This means we're imprisoned by economic growth, imprisoned in the spiral of money and interest.

Money is a mode of organizing our life in the material world; money is an invention, a mental device, very necessary, very ingenious, but in the end, a product of the mind.
  – Jacob Needleman

2 MONEY: MEANS OR END?

If I borrow a crate of apples from you because the harvest from my tree has failed, you expect to get a crate of apples in return after the next harvest. Or you might get a few bales of hay from me in the meantime. For centuries, humanity has functioned very well with this system. Money was initially intended to simplify the process – to be used if there didn't happen to be any apples or bales of hay. Money was a means. Then somebody decided that if you lend ten ducats, you could demand eleven in return. No one ever demanded eleven apples if he had made a loan of ten. But with money it was different: interest was born, and not without any resistance. Religion was fiercely opposed to it. Judaism, Christianity and Islam all explicitly prohibit charging interest. The Jews quickly found a way out, however. The Old Testament says, "Thou shall not lend upon usury to thy *brother.*" The next verse explicitly states that you may charge interest to *strangers*, so the Jews charged interest to non-Jews. In Europe, interest was first legalized in 1545 by Henry VIII after breaking with the Pope of Rome. The Catholic Church continued to oppose interest until the nineteenth century. Today, only mullahs in mosques object to interest. A rearguard action, we say to ourselves. Interest is generally accepted, and no one can imagine a world without it.

Yet opposing interest isn't such a strange idea. No other system in our modern economy, after all, is so disruptive. Interest forces the emergence of competition as well as endless economic growth. Say I borrow 200,000 euros for a mortgage. The bank expects me to pay back about 400,000 euros over the next twenty years. Otherwise I lose my house. That extra 200,000 euros has to come from somewhere. We could just print it – but we know that's a bad idea. So someone else has to forfeit it. This isn't just true for my mortgage. The same applies to all the mortgages in the entire world, and for every other kind of loan. This explains the gigantic competition today, and it explains why Darwin's survival theory was so easily adapted in political and social circles. Everyone experiences this competition every day. The system of interest means that somebody else has to go bankrupt to make it possible for me to keep my house. Somebody has to lose his 200,000 euros so that I can pay my 200,000-euro interest payment.

Or the economy grows. More money comes in so more people can make their interest payments. In that case, the interest rate determines the level of economic growth. If there isn't enough growth, more bankruptcies occur. It's as simple as that. And in the end there can never be enough growth because the arithmetic progression of interest on interest exceeds all reality. If today I deposit one euro in the bank, in a thousand years that euro will have grown to a sum with about fifty zeroes. Or if Joseph and Mary had deposited one cent in the bank for their son at four percent interest in the year 0, their descendents in 1749 would have been entitled to a golden ball weighing as much as the earth. And in 1990 that capital would have equaled more than eight thousand golden earths. In other words, matter can never keep up with interest. This is why linking money to gold – the gold standard – was finally abandoned for good in 1971. Modern money is not linked to matter but to debts – more and more debts (to be dealt with in the next chapter). But this still doesn't resolve the tension between interest and economic growth. Interest still incites the rise of debilitating competition. Interest cannot be sustained without continuous economic growth – with all the corresponding negative consequences for humanity and nature. In addition, interest results in the concentration of wealth in the hands of a few at the expense of the masses. Interest leads to inequality. If you already have money, it's easier to get more money than if you have no money at all. Interest works "for nothing" for the rich, while the poor always have to make an enormous effort to build up capital. Studies show that more money always ends up in the hands of those who already have it. This accounts for the insane situation in which the three richest billionaires in the world have more money than the combined gross national product of the world's fifty poorest countries. It's an intolerable state of affairs. You can understand why religions opposed interest for so long. You can also understand why the system of wealth redistribution by means of multi-level taxing developed during the same period as the legalization of interest.

Finally, interest is an obstacle to useful progress. Interest determines the profitability of every investment. Say I invest 1,000 euros in a solar panel that will save me 100 euros annually in electricity bills over the next fifteen years. This seems like a splendid bit of number work: I spend 1,000 euros and I get 1,500 back, which means in fifteen years I make a 500-euro profit – half my investment. In the world of interest, however, there's nothing splendid about it. If I put my 1,000 euros in the bank instead, I'll have at least 3,000 euros after fifteen years, thanks to interest. So my investment in the solar panel is absolutely not cost-effective. The same number work applies to countless other economic activities – they're only cost-effective if they beat the "automatic" profit that comes from interest. This also accounts for the pressure and the stress.

In our complex modern society, in which very few people still own their own apple trees, no one can survive without money. Everything revolves around money. And the kind of money we have determines the kind of society we live in. So we now live in a society of competition, imposed economic growth and a concentration of wealth, a society in which profit and interest play tag and businesses don't get a chance to look any further than the next quarter. In this merry-go-round, you soon forget that the current system of money and interest is nothing but a choice – an "ingenious invention," according to the statement by philosopher Jacob Needleman quoted at the beginning of the chapter. But fascinating experiments have been made with other forms of money that have an entirely different effect on human relations.

One of the most striking historical examples concerns the system devised by Silvio Gesell, an Argentinean-German businessman. Gesell was minister of finances for the republic of Bavaria for a short time in 1918. He got rid of the interest system because it provided extra rewards for those with money without their having to do anything to get it. Gesell therefore proposed a system of negative interest, whereby people would be charged for the use of money, the way they were charged for the use of electricity or the telephone. The longer you held onto money, the more you would have to pay. Extensive experiments were carried out with this system in villages in southern Germany and Austria during the Depression years, between 1924 and 1934. One such place was the Austrian village of Wörgl, with a population of 4,500. At the beginning of the 1930s, Wörgl had a high unemployment rate. Many families didn't have a penny to spend. There was plenty of work to be done – a great deal of overdue maintenance of the streets and water works – but no money to pay for it. So the village council distributed 5,500 new, interest-free schillings. On the back of each bill were twelve boxes. After a month, the validity of each bill could be extended with a stamp from the city – at a charge of one percent of the value of the bill. So a 100-schilling bill would be stamped after a month and would become a 99-schilling bill. This "users' tax" stimulated the population to spend money to avoid having to pay for the money they owned at the end of the month. Saving was thereby discouraged, but investing was rewarded. So the inhabitants of Wörgl paid their bills, taxes and loans as quickly as possible, and merchants were generous in extending credit to each other. Unemployment dropped from more than 30 percent to a marginal level. Houses were restored, roads improved and water pipes modernized. A plaque on the town bridge proudly recalls the episode: "This bridge was built with our own free money." And the revenue from the users' tax was used to finance a community soup kitchen.

This activity extended well beyond the village council's list of overdue maintenance projects. The circulation of the new schilling began with payments to people working for the village, but the money was quickly distributed via these few to the other inhabitants. In the fourteen months between July 1932 and November 1933, the 5,500 new schillings changed owners 416 times, making it possible to pay for economic activities valued at about 2.5 million schillings. The new schilling created over ten times more employment than the ordinary interest-bearing Austrian currency, which just sat in the bank. In other words, interest-bearing money creates scarcity and interest-free money stimulates activity.

Wörgl's success attracted attention. Two hundred other Austrian villages followed suit. The French prime minister, Edouard Dalladier, came to visit. But in 1934 the Austrian central bank claimed its authority was being undermined and succeeded in getting the Supreme Court in Vienna to declare the experiments illegal. It was cold comfort for Gesell to learn that John Maynard Keynes, in his *General Theory* written during the same period, stated that the system worked. More than that, he predicated, "The future would learn more from Gesell than from Marx."

We're almost a century further on, and Keynes's prediction is yet to be proven true. Even so, the spirit of Gesell is abroad in more than 2000 complementary monetary systems operating all over the world: in New Zealand, Australia, the United States, Canada and the European Union. A system like this gets started when a community agrees to use a different kind of currency as its means of exchange – as happened in Wörgl. It was the Canadian Michael Linton who blew new life into these complementary monetary systems in the early 1980s. He introduced the *Local Exchange Trading System* (Lets). A Lets system creates a local, parallel economy without any monetary deficit. The members of a Lets system extend services to each other which are settled (partially) by means of i.e. "green euros." For example: Anne has Charles, a plumber, repair a leaky roof in her home. She pays Charles 40 green euros for his work, plus 15 euros for a new tap. Then Anne goes to the hairdresser, where she pays 30 green euros and 10 euros for shampoo and a hairbrush. Anne raises vegetables in her garden, and she makes a deal with her neighbor Carla whereby she will furnish her with vegetables for 30 green euros. She provides vegetables to another neighbor, Harry, for 20 green euros.

The ordinary euros are paid immediately in cash. The transactions made in green euros are reported on the website of the Lets system. Anne's total bill ends up looking like this: she has bought goods and services at a value of 95 euros, but she only has to pay 25 euros in cash. In addition, she still has a 20-euro debt in the Lets system, which she can pay off with vegetable deliveries, for instance. Lets is more than bartering. By using the system website, Anne can pay off her 20-green euro debt to anyone in the Lets group. It isn't necessary to come up with an exact fit of reciprocal needs. This is why the green euros are real money. In a Lets system, there is never a shortage of money; money is created as soon as people agree to trade with each other. There is no interest that plays people off against each other. On the contrary, Lets stimulates cooperation and strengthens mutual relationships.

Michael Linton's Lets system has made its way all over the world. And there are other, comparable systems. "Time-money," for instance, which is calculated in hours. Peter works one hour in Christine's garden, and he can use this hour to have John polish his car. Ithaca, a town with a population of 27,000 in upstate New York in the United States, uses a refined version of the time-money system. Twice a month, a newspaper comes out in which inhabitants and local companies can advertise their willingness to accept "Ithaca hours." The "hour" is based on a minimum hourly wage of ten dollars. There are 1,200 individuals participating in the system and 200 companies, which include a supermarket, movie theaters, lawyers and restaurants. The newspaper prints everything on offer, which is a combination of ordinary dollars and Ithaca hours. A plumber advertises that he is available for 15 dollars an hour, 80-20. That means that will accept 80 percent of his fee in Ithaca hours. A movie theater or restaurant might accept 100 percent Ithaca hours during the lunch hour – when there are fewer customers anyway. In that case, the movie theater or restaurant is faced with the choice of an empty chair or an occupied chair paid for with Ithaca hours. So the establishment builds up a credit in Ithaca hours in addition to its regular turnover, which it can use to obtain certain services – the window washer, for instance.

In Japan there's a "health currency." Volunteers who care for a sick or aged person build up credit which they or their family or friends can use to get similar care. Systems like this can be quite extensive in size. In Switzerland, the national complementary system, WIR, has existed since 1934. It has 80,000 members and currently has an annual turnover of about 2.5 billion Swiss francs. A modern variant of a complementary system is the airmiles or frequent flyer programs. Initially these programs were no more than a commercial relationship between the airline and its passengers. Now these systems have developed into a "currency" that can be traded at the gas station or in the supermarket as well. The significance of such alternative systems of payment will only increase because they are methods companies use to try to hold on to their customers. The more a company can offer a customer with its stamps or airmiles – that is, if more can be purchased than airline tickets – the more interesting for the customer that company becomes. In this way, interest in the complementary monetary system also increases. It's going to become easier and easier to exchange complementary currencies for real euros or dollars. If you can exchange rubles for dollars, then why not airmiles for dollars?

Airmiles are pointing the way to the future of complementary systems. Such systems are potentially much more than "old-fashioned bartering played by well-intentioned hippie idealists." The skepticism is disappearing, and governments in New Zealand, Australia, the states of the US and the countries of the European Union are actively contributing to the creation of such systems. Even the attitude of the central banks is changing. The central bank of New Zealand, for instance, was the first to openly admit that complementary monetary systems help curb inflation. In systems like these, someone can only gain a credit if someone else has a debit to balance it out. The sum of all these activities is zero – the amount of money remains the same. But in the meantime countless houses have been painted, gardens maintained and cars repaired. In other words, economic needs are fulfilled without requiring extra money. Complementary systems make transactions possible that would not otherwise have taken place. This, then, is evidence of *more* economic activity. Complementary systems prevent society from becoming crippled by lack of money. It's insane that, as so often happens, a widely-acknowledged need arises (refurbishing a school, for instance), an eager workforce is at hand, but because there's no money available the job never gets done.

Complementary systems also stimulate reciprocity and cooperation. They strengthen the community. And that produces yet another amazing effect: better health. A health insurance company in the United States charges lower premiums to participants in a Lets group in Brooklyn, New York, because the company has discovered that those people are sick less often. In addition, complementary systems can serve as vital instruments in financing local commercial activity. The systems help small businesses compete against the onslaught of big store chains. Local enterprises can make much better use of local goods and services than the chains, which do large-scale centralized purchasing. This is an important advantage for the community because it's not the big chains but the small, local businesses that are the main source of employment. A complementary system can also help finance a new small business. The fact is that a small company has much more difficulty obtaining a bank loan than a new branch of a well-known international franchise. Say I need money because I want to open a café. I distribute 120 euro's worth of vouchers that the customer can spend in my café. The customer pays 100 euros for these vouchers, giving him a 20 percent discount. But if my costs amount to 40 euros, I'm still earning 60 euros from my customer. So we both benefit: I have financing and a loyal customer, and my customer enjoys a discount that he would not be given in another café.

The economic value of complementary systems is far-reaching and can easily exceed the local examples given here. In his recent book *The Future of Money*, the Belgian banker Bernhard Lietaer proposes the introduction of a worldwide complementary monetary system – the *terra*. The terra consists of a shopping basket of commodities (oil, grain, copper, gold, etc.). The portion of commodities contained in the terra is determined by the portion of those same commodities in world trade. The value of the terra equals the value of the basket of commodities and is listed daily in the financial pages. The terra also actually entitles its owner to the underlying commodities. You can regard the new currency as a coupon that can be used to pick up commodities from the "terra repository." Each year, the owner of the terra pays about three percent of the value of his commodities in storage costs. Those costs are comparable to Silvio Gesell's negative interest, and they stimulate the terra owner to spend his terras.

The initiative to introduce the terra would have to be taken by the multinational business community. But as soon as the terra were put into circulation, every world citizen could use it as a means of exchange. The business community has much more influence on the economy today than governments, and businesses also suffer more from fluctuations in the rates of exchange characterizing the current financial markets. The fluctuations that plague world trade are to a great extent a consequence of the dropping of the gold standard in 1971, when the relationship between the financial and the physical world was broken. The terra restores that relationship. The need for stability is readily apparent in the rapid growth of bartering. The value of bartering that is going on today is an estimated one trillion dollars. Of the 500 largest companies, two out of three are regularly involved in bartering.

The terra is not vulnerable to inflation. Inflation is defined as a change in the price of a certain amount of products and services. But with the terra, price changes also lead to changes in world trade (if oil becomes more expensive, then more trading is done in coal), causing the ratio of commodities in the terra shopping basket to change. The terra contributes to a stable world economy in other ways, too. If a recession threatens and a surplus of commodities forms, companies will want to sell their commodities for terras. They will then want to spend these terras as quickly as possible to avoid paying storage costs. In this way, the terra stimulates economic activity just when the prevailing economy is getting bogged down. Or from the other way around, if the economy is running at top speed, the terra helps put the brakes on economic activity. In this case, businesses will want to exchange more terras for commodities. That means fewer terras will come into circulation, reducing economic activity.

The stimulation and introduction of complementary monetary systems would have a salutary effect on the world economy. This is not to say that such systems are a balm for every known economic problem. Some investments demand massive amounts of money. You can't build a steel mill with a Lets group, for instance. But when it comes down to a more humane economy, the introduction of complementary systems, in addition to the national currency, is useful and relevant. Complementary systems foster activities and social functions in a way that euros do not. They break through the destructive cycle of interest and profit. Every day, we read about central bankers making desperate attempts to restrain the rampant flow of money in the world. But no one can put the genie of interest back in the bottle. The system we have chosen, with its money and interest, determines how we invest, do business and live. Within that system, money has become an end in itself – often at the expense of people and nature. By introducing a new monetary system, in which money is a means and no interest is charged, the reforming of the world economy can begin. In the end, money is a means for serving our lives.

Seven million children die each year because money is spent on debt payments instead of health and clean water.
   – Jubilee 2000 coalition

3 PERNICIOUS DEBTS

On the editorial staff where I made my start as a rookie economics journalist, there was one respected senior member who specialized in "debts." It was the early 1980s, and Mexico, Argentina and Brazil were taking turns throwing the international financial world into a turmoil. You got used to seeing serious bankers appear on the front pages or in news broadcasts with their predictions of doom. The Middle East, nuclear weapons *and* the debt crisis – that was the news during those years. One morning, one of the chief editors, searching for an opening for the daily paper, approached the "debt editor" with a press release from yet another alarmed banker who was worried about Mexico's failure to honor its interest and repayment obligations. My colleague was a down-to-earth Dutchman from the south who was not easily flustered, certainly not by Third World debts. I can still hear his answer, spoken almost twenty years ago: "If the developing countries actually did pay their debts, those bankers would really have a problem."

Bingo. Banks live from debts – from interest. All their whining notwithstanding, they'd be in big trouble if every country, business and individual paid their debts and didn't come back to borrow more. What's worse – debts are the precondition for today's world economy. That's right. Debt – what every right-minded person tries to get out of – is of crucial importance for our daily lives. We have organized the economy in such a way that we cannot live without debt.

Debts are everywhere. My fellow debt editor wrote about the debts of the Third World, but all rich countries have debts, too. The Dutch national debt is almost 230 billion euros, the German debt is almost 300 billion euros, the Japanese is two trillion dollars and the American is five trillion dollars. No country is debt-free. But it doesn't stop there. The indebtedness of businesses and private individuals is also enormous, and it's constantly growing. Think especially of the mortgages of homeowners. The total mortgage debt of Dutch homeowners in 1998 was almost 200 billion euros. The reason those debts are so important is because almost all the debt money goes into circulation. You may think that money is created by the state, that coins are minted and bank notes are printed under the government's responsibility. Actually, less than five percent of all money enters the economy that way. More than 95 percent of the total amount of money consists of mere figures and is created by banks through loans. Almost every euro goes into circulation because someone has taken out a loan. Once upon a time, a bank could only extend a loan if a similar amount of money existed in savings. But if someone wants to apply for credit today, he's never told, "We're sorry, there's no money available for loans at the moment." For a new line of credit the bank simply "makes" new money as long as the borrower satisfies the terms of the bank. And if someone takes out a mortgage, it doesn't mean someone else's purchasing power is curtailed. No, it means extra new purchasing power is created. In this way the daily advance of debts continues.

We find ourselves in a peculiar cycle. Economic activity depends on money. Money is created almost exclusively by dept. That means economic activity depends on debt. No debts means no money, which means economic stagnation. Citizens wrestle with mortgages, business with their credit rating and governments with the national debt – and all this to keep the economy afloat.

Except for the few coins and notes that the government puts into circulation, all the money is "debt money." This has serious consequences, because banks that "make" money want to be paid for it. They want to receive interest, or to make sure the amount of money keeps growing at a satisfactory rate to provide that interest. So more people, businesses and countries have to incur more debts. It's a slavery of indebtedness from which almost no one escapes. And almost no one is allowed to escape, because the existence of debts is essential. A paid-off mortgage must be replaced by a new debt as quickly as possible, or the economy will have no money. Every now and then someone manages to pull out unscathed, someone buys her or his house with his own money without taking out a loan. But all those individuals together do not possess as much money as the total amount of all the mortgages in the world. And wealthy businesses are only wealthy on paper because their property is worth much more than their debts. Our reality is controlled by debts.

It's incredible, but the prudent consumer is a danger to the economy. If all consumers only bought what they could afford and paid off their mortgages, a large part of the business community would go bankrupt. Incomes would drop, prices would rise and people would be forced to take on new debts to put money into circulation. It also doesn't matter how efficiently companies produce, how successful they are in keeping their costs down, how inexpensively they manufacture, how shrewdly they merge – the debts have to continue. Without an alternative way to create money, a stable economy is unconceivable.

The ever-growing burden of debt is harmful to the economy. Debts force the economy to grow so that interest and installment payments can be financed. The employer feels that pressure when he has to pay his mortgage, which is why he's not quick to switch to a more satisfying job with lower pay. Forced by the same pressure, companies produce more and more new, low-quality products that have to be replaced rapidly. It makes no difference if new products are needed or not. The bottom line is that without new investments there can be no new debts, so no new money enters the economy, resulting in recession. In short, the need is for all those new investments – for money – and not for all the new products.

Debts make money scarce. The money is constantly being pulled in two directions. On the one hand it's needed to support the trade in products and services, and on the other hand it's needed to pay off debts. This explains the chronic shortage of money, which keeps competition in a constant state of stimulation. This money shortage is also evident in the fact that the total sum of all available income in the world is never enough to pay for all the products being offered for sale. A consoling balance doesn't exist in today's economy. Paradoxically enough, this lack of balance is the very factor that forces new products and services to be brought into the world. Every new company gets started by making investments. A new publisher begins to pay salaries. This causes the total income in the economy to rise, so new products can be bought. But that improvement takes time. Then the publisher puts its books on the market in an attempt to earn back the salaries it has paid out – its investment – through the price of the books. This is possible only at the expense of other products because there is no additional source of income. The temporary "solution" is to start up another company that also begins investing and also goes into debt. You can see this dance of debt in the "credit sales" that are flooding the economy right now, and in the remarkable fact that someone today can spend twenty years paying off his mortgage on a house that was built decades or even centuries ago.

There will be no peace in the economy – and in the lives of human individuals – until there is sufficient money in circulation to enable them to purchase the products and services now on offer without having to go into debt to do it. This sounds like asking for a miracle, but there is a simple intervention that would make it possible: the steady introduction of debt-free money, such as the money made available through the complementary monetary systems described in the previous chapter. In his book *The Grip of Death*, Michael Rowbothom argues for the introduction of a guaranteed minimum income, not as a gauge of the social welfare state, with which we are already familiar, but as a means of paying off debts. If the government creates more money, the need for loans is reduced, so fewer debts are incurred. This smacks of inflation. Let's just assume that extra money is created. This is accomplished either by the banks – and then it's debt money, or by the government – and then it's debt-free money. The debt-free government money enters the economy via government investments and via the guaranteed minimum income. Rowbothom reasons that if people had more money to spend, there would be fewer demands for wage increases. In addition, this reinforcement of purchasing power would enable companies to sell their products at prices that would help them pay their debts. In short, the creation of money by the government entails no extra costs, helps pay off old debts and reduces the demand for higher wages. But when banks create money it means that businesses or consumers have to go into debt, and that leads to salary demands and higher prices. So which is more inflation sensitive, Rowbothom asks, "debt money" or "debt-free money"? The author demonstrates that with a well-considered policy – an annual guaranteed minimum income of a few thousands guilders for each citizen – a reasonable balance could be achieved between "debt money" and "debt-free money" in a period of about twenty years. The national debt and the mortgages would then be paid off and there would be plenty of money for trade. This does not mean that loans would no longer exist. It only means that the economy would have freed itself from the deadly grip of debt.

A special approach is needed for the debts of the developing nations. In those countries, the modern economy's dance of debt has been most insidious. The wealthy countries, Western businesses and mortgage owners can at least carry on in the debt economy – even though a more wholesome path does exist. But the developing countries are hopelessly swept along in this insanity. The Third World has paid off its debt many times over, but because of the "interest on interest" effect their debt is now bigger than ever.

   The idea behind the debts owed by developing countries is simple. A country approaches the International Monetary Fund (IMF) or the World Bank and asks for a loan to finance a project intended to promote economic development in that country – export in particular. The basic idea is that the financed project will result in products that can be exported. And the profit from that export can then be used to pay off the loan. Nice model, but it's never worked. Brazil – which represents one of the success stories! – saw its gross national product quadruple between 1960 and 1980, but after those twenty years it found itself saddled with a much larger foreign debt. In 1990, Brazil reached the point at which the total proceeds from export was still not enough to satisfy debt obligations. Many developing countries find themselves in the same situation. There are countries today whose net annual payment to the IMF and the World Bank is greater than what they receive in support. In the period 1992-1998, Ghana paid 560 million dollars more to the IMF than it received in new loans and credits. Among the consequences: Ghana can only afford to pay 7 dollars a year per inhabitant for health care (the Netherlands: 1,500 dollars).

The export model has failed utterly. The income from export has not been sufficient to pay off the debts – not even when a particular project is successful. In addition, the urge to export has been seriously damaging to the development of national economies. Developing countries now produce apples for Western countries when apples in those wealthy nations are out of season. It's no wonder that domestic food production suffers with priorities like these. Thanks to the ruinous policy of the IMF and the World Bank, more and more countries are forced to purchase their own food – food that they once produced themselves – from Western multinational corporations. And then there's the environmental damage that the chemical monoculture has inflicted on their agricultural land. And the scandalous policy of "tied aid" in which countries are compelled to earmark their loans for purchases in the donor countries, and not, for instance, in other neighboring developing countries.

The export model was doomed to failure, because when the developing countries enter the world market with their products for export, whom do they encounter? Exactly – *all* the other countries of the world (and that's including the rich countries, which have debts, too, and are trying to pay them off with extra income from export). An export war is raging on the world market. Developing countries participate in the struggle, but they're lagging far behind. No one denies that they're *developing* countries. So Ghana and Bangladesh start exporting goods with which the market is already glutted, goods that in most cases can be better produced by other countries. An additional consequence of this unequal trade situation is that the currencies of the developing countries are continually being devaluated. When devaluation occurs, more and more money is needed to pay off debts. An example with fictitious figures: Pakistan borrowed a million dollars twenty years ago. At the time, that would have been, say, 10 million rupees.

During those twenty years, the Pakistani rupee has dropped in value by a factor of ten. This means that the debt – apart from the interest – is now 100 million rupees. So Pakistan has to pay back ten times more than it borrowed. There are all sorts of financial tricks today, such as *hedging*, that Western pension funds use to cover themselves against these kinds of losses, but dodges like these aren't used for Third World debts. At the mercy of the crippled export model, developing countries are handed over to the whims of the financial markets. Even if you contend that it's quite normal for a country to pay back its loans – and generally speaking that is true – you can't get around the flagrant injustice of the existing situation. The debts of the Third World have not been "normal" for quite some time.

In the meantime, developing countries take out new loans in order to finance their interest and payment obligations from the old debts. This is like being unable to pay your mortgage and solving the problem by taking out another loan. It's called a bottomless pit. If this happens to an individual or a company, they go bankrupt. There are laws that apply to this situation. But these rules do not apply to countries and international organizations. It should be possible for developing countries to go bankrupt and to start all over again. The strangling export model renders their starting position hopeless. But countries cannot go bankrupt. Their debts go on forever, even when the signs of bankruptcy are reflected in the child mortality rate – every week 130,000 children die as a result of these debts – in erosion, in pollution, in the slums and the destruction of communities, in the destruction of life itself. It is hardly edifying to ponder the fact that the money created by Third World debts keeps the economies of rich countries afloat, a fact that makes accomplices of us all.

Without a bankruptcy law for countries, the debt crisis threatens to keep on festering. Or does it? If there are no laws, then the

Bible – O paradox – offers help. That's the source of inspiration for the Jubilee 2000 campaign, for canceling the debts of the poorest countries. In the book of Leviticus, chapter 25, we read that God created the world to live in harmony. Once every seven years, all creditors were to give their debtors a "repayment holiday." Once every seven times seven years there was to be a "jubilee year" in which all debts would be canceled, slaves would be set free and people who had lost their land because of debts would return to it. Elsewhere in the Bible there is confirmation of this "jubilee" celebration in Leviticus. The idea was that rich property owners would be reminded that "their" property ultimately belonged to God, and that the growth of riches went hand in hand with social responsibilities. This harmony was to be restored once every 49 years.

Canceling debts does not solve the problem of poverty in the world. But it is a beginning, and it also reminds us that money does not exist apart from the community – from the human individual. Creditors really do have more responsibility than making sure they are paid back. It is significant of the lost state of modern capitalism that it takes Leviticus to remind us of this.

If the debt of the Third World were canceled, developing countries would be able to focus once again on the development of their own economies – their agriculture, infrastructure and industry – within their own cultures. These countries would be able to admit foreign investment on their own terms. And they would be able to participate in world trade according to their own priorities – knowing that they possess, say, the raw materials so badly needed by rich countries. Freed from debt, a much more equitable trade could emerge.

While eliminating nationalism is indeed a good idea, the elimination of sovereignty is not.
  – Paul Hawken

4 EXPORT WAR

I always used to think free trade was a noble pursuit, perhaps because free trade sounds so much like freedom itself. A world with open borders, international cooperation, a united, federal Europe – to me they seemed like nothing less than elements for a better future. You might say I got my wish. The process of globalization now taking place in the world appears to be a success for internationalists. We're watching the world become one. Even so, I've lost my initial enthusiasm. Free trade has not brought what I had hoped it would. What went wrong?

Every story about trade begins with Adam Smith. This eighteenth-century British founder of the science of economics explained that if everyone concentrated on their own specialty, the result would be the best for all concerned. In applying this principle to factories, a company is more productive if all the employees aren't involved in manufacturing the entire product, but if different employees or departments specialize in the production of parts. The same is true for countries. The English climate is more suited to raising sheep than growing grapes. In Portugal it's just the other way around. If England concentrates on wool production and Portugal on grape cultivation for wine, both countries are sticking to what they do best. The English export their wool surplus to Portugal and import surplus Portuguese wine. International trade increases because countries export the products they can make most economically and import what other countries can make more economically. According to Smith's theory, specialization leads to more efficiency, more productivity and more prosperity. His ideal was an open world in which goods and services could move freely. Countries should not strive towards self-sufficiency, but should specialize in the production of those things for which they enjoy "comparative cost advantages," as they're called. If everything is then produced in the most economical way, everyone is better off. The "invisible hand" of the market points every employee, every company and even every country – based on their own enlightened interests – in the most beneficial direction for the world economy as a whole.

An excellent theory, as far as it goes. The fact that reality turned out to be more unruly cannot be laid at Smith's door. In his day, it was obvious that progress would best be served if everyone did not bake his own bread but left that task to the specialists – "bakers." The theory breaks down right from the start because of the total absence of equal trading partners. Even in Adam Smith's time, commercial success was wholly dependent on whether a country possessed a powerful fleet or not, and military strength has little to do with economics. Today, an American product has an easier time making its way in world trade than a product from Zambia.

What Smith could not have predicted is that in our day, money moves around the world as freely as goods. The free circulation of capital completely undermines his theory. In the modern world, English pounds flow to Portugal if wine can thereby be produced in an attractive way. But this means that English money is not available to the English wool industry. In addition, seventy percent of today's world trade is in the hands of 500 multinational corporations. These corporations exploit local advantages in their own way, to the benefit of their own shareholders and not to the benefit of their own countries, and they obscure the picture of countries working together to share their strongest sides. The trade you see today has little to do with Smith's vision. Video recorders from Singapore are unloaded in Rotterdam Harbor, while at the same time video recorders from the Netherlands are being hauled off the ships in the harbor of Singapore. In Paris, Renaults, Peugeots and Citroëns are put on the train bound for Germany, and the same train returns to France loaded with BMWs, Mercedes and Opels. Apples from Chile are stocked in Dutch supermarkets along with apples from orchards in the Netherlands. Unilever buys milk powder from New Zealand for the production of food products in Dutch factories that are located right next to pastures where Dutch cows graze. Dutch pigs are shipped to Italy and come back as Parma ham. Adam Smith wouldn't know what to make of it – but I don't either. Comparative cost advantages are few and far between in this circus.

It gets even worse. Trade suggests reciprocity, the concerted action of importing and exporting. But that's not what is going on. The globalization now taking place is one big export war. Each country is trying to finance its national debt (see the previous chapter) through export. Not one country is interested in an equal balance of trade. Whether it's the United States, Germany, Spain or Japan, or Ethiopia, Uganda, Paraguay or Sri Lanka – each country wants the same thing: a trade surplus. Each country wants to export more than it imports. Each country is openly aiming for imbalance, not for reciprocity. Each country is launching simultaneous export attacks on all the other countries under the guise of united progress. This is more like war than trade, which is reflected in modern economic parlance: markets are "penetrated" and "defended."

There's no way that all the countries can reach their goal. For every country with a trade surplus there is by definition another country with a trade deficit. There are winners and there are losers, with no sign of the "distribution of talent" whereby all participants win. The most painful aspect of this export struggle is that even the winners are actually losers. A country that exports more than it imports is constantly losing labor and energy to other countries – more goes out than comes in. That loss may indeed be compensated for with money but it's a human loss all the same, which explains why so many people find they have to work harder and harder. Neither does this loss seem to entail any reciprocal advantage. After all, the idea was that the quality of life in England would improve if people specialized in wool production, whereas wine production – less suitable for England and therefore more difficult and tedious – would be left to Portugal. Two bicyclists racing side by side who take turns giving each other the advantage both cycle faster with less effort. But that system doesn't work if one of the two bicyclists only wants to be ahead. In that case, the cyclist in the lead may be ahead, but he loses more energy. He experiences no gains except perhaps for the medal – the money – when, battle-weary, he crosses the finish line.

Politicians always present free trade as a "win-win" system for all concerned, whereas in practice none of those gains are ever recovered. It is reported that thanks to the European Union, the North American trade agreement NAFTA and other agreements, world prosperity has risen. But these are one-sided figures. The big trade blocs have been able to carry on the export war more successfully, at the expense of developing countries. The difference in incomes between the richest and the poorest twenty percent of the world population is two and a half times bigger than it was in 1960. Eighty-six percent of the goods in the world go to the wealthiest twenty percent of the world's citizens. The poorest twenty percent get one percent. It's hard to imagine how the ideal of free trade – with its obvious shortcomings – could have been pursued unrestrained for so long. And we haven't even started to address the threat that free trade forms for public health, the environment and respect for human rights.

Since 1995, the World Trade Organization (WTO) has functioned as the watchdog for protecting free trade. In practice, this
means that the policy of governments wanting to protect the environment or public health, governments that have passed laws to
prohibit or restrict the importing of products considered polluting or harmful, is overridden by binding pronouncements from
the WTO. The WTO has shaken the American clean air legisla-
tion by allowing the Venezuelan oil industry to sell polluted gaso-
line in the United States. Likewise, no impediments may be placed
in the international trade in waste products, and as a result dangerous waste is being dumped in developing countries. No distinctions may be made in production and development methods.
Tuna that are caught in "dolphin-friendly" nets must be treated
the same as tuna caught in nets that ensnare dolphins. Europe may
not grant preferential treatment to small-scale banana importers
in former European colonies in the Caribbean and thereby pass
over large American multinationals, such as Chiquita. And the
WTO isn't even disturbed about the large-scale infertility among
banana pickers on the plantations of the large producers as a result
of working with excessive amounts of pesticides. In Honduras
children are being born with serious birth defects, but free trade
must go on. In other words, attempts to protect people, public
health and the environment are condemned as "protectionism."
The World Trade Organization will not allow countries to set their
own standards, to express independent values or to decide what
they will or will not support – and all this mainly in the interest
of those 500 multinational corporations that account for three-
quarters of the world's trade. This is no longer free trade; it's trade
driven by the stock exchange, concentrating more and more power in fewer hands of fewer companies. Mongolia wants to participate in world trade, so it has become a member of the WTO. As

a result, the Mongolians have no choice but to allow a Pizza Hut to be built in Ulan Bator.

It's no wonder that this free trade is losing public support. The meeting of the WTO in Seattle in November 1999 was a turning point. That meeting came to a standstill as a result of protest by tens of thousands of people from all over the world. The media reported a battle with the police. The newspapers were full of photos of burning vehicles and stone-throwing demonstrators. But of far more interest was the breadth of the resistance. In addition to the familiar "professional" hot-heads there were writers, scientists and "ordinary" citizens passing through the streets of Seattle. They showed that globalization in the interest of multinational corporations did not have their support. Nine out of ten Britons think the government should protect citizen from multinationals when it comes to employment, care for the environment, public health, etc. Viewed from this perspective, it's ironic that members of parliament often don't even know what treaties they're ratifying. Treaties such as NAFTA and the European Union cover a lot of policy territory but are read by only a few. The well-known American activist and recent presidential candidate Ralph Nader promised to contribute 10,000 dollars to a worthy cause if any member of Congress could prove to him that he had read the 550 pages of the so-called Uruguay Round trade agreement and was prepared to answer a few questions. One Republican congressman accepted the challenge... changed his opinion and consequently voted against it.

Opposition to the WTO and globalization is not opposition to trade. As I write this, I'm drinking a cup of tea. A Dutchman can't drink a cup of tea without trade. I like to eat oranges, but they don't grow in my garden. The American author and professor Herman Daly pointed out the difference between international trade and the process of globalization that is now underway. Globalization is about uniform regulations, about a world in which goods and money can move around without individual countries having any say in the matter. Internationalization means trade between countries. Those countries determine their own standards, and it is up to the other countries to decide if they want to do business or not. Naturally, it has been shown that these opportunities were sometimes exploited in the past. And naturally, countries have been known to conceal crude protectionist aims behind "noble" regulations. But when it comes to democracy, countries and their inhabitants ought to be able to set their own policy. The alternative is a world trade organization in which not a single citizen has any influence and which therefore can never enjoy broad support.

The question asked by the WTO is: what uniform regulations should apply to world trade? A better question would be: how can trade regulations be drawn up so that different cultures, nations and countries are treated most fairly? Because right now there are enormous differences: there's very little in Germany to attract a Vietnamese bank, whereas German banks open branches all over the world. And what does Mongolia have to offer in response to the arrival of a Pizza Hut? You might compare the unequal starting points in world trade with taxation inside national borders. It's generally accepted that someone who earns more pays more taxes. We pay taxes according to our ability to pay, as it's called. Similarly, you should be able to participate in world trade "according to your ability to pay." This means that Honduras should be able to protect its economy more than the United States. It also means that Pizza Hut should not be allowed to go to Ulan Bator, but the Mongolians should be free to export their hides to Europe. Isn't that justice? Free trade can only be pursued if there is equality for everyone involved. The simple removal of trade impediments is no solution for the problem concealed behind those impediments. Those impediments were set up as protection against aggressive export competition. As long as every country is weighed down by huge foreign debts, and as long as they finance those debts through export, protective regulations will remain in place as an urgent necessity.

In his book *Localization*, Colin Hines presents localization as an alternative for globalization. Localization means a policy for discriminating in favor of local production and trade. Such a policy would support the community and reduce inequality, while serving the environment through local participation. Multinational corporations have no local interests, which is clearly to the detriment of the communities in which they establish themselves – often temporarily. Protective regulations may be involved within the context of localization. This is not protectionism, since protectionism is closing off your own markets while you expect others to keep their markets open for you. This is quite different from protective regulations, which serve localization around the world. Localization goes hand in hand with internationalization – a free exchange of technology, ideas and information. Localization leads to international cooperation rather than incapacitating competition and large-scale pollution. Think of all that unnecessary transportation for the senseless trade in cars and video recorders that characterizes modern globalization. Within the current regime of the World Trade Organization, a country is obliged to treat the products from another country just as it treats the same product made domestically. Hines goes on to adapt this regulation: the limitation of trade is encouraged in support of local employment and protection of the environment and the consumer. The new principle applying to trade between countries stipulates that trade must not undermine local production. In addition, countries may expect their trading partners to provide fair working conditions and to show respect for human rights and for the environment.

Hand in hand, localization and internationalization will bring human beings back into the economy and into world trade. This may mean monetary loss, but I think it's an acceptable price to pay. People would be served, but so would democracy and nature. And trade could begin to reflect the cooperation and reciprocity that once were, and hopefully will remain, its ideal – for me, in any case.

My proposal is to throw some sand in the wheels of our excessively efficient international money markets.
  – James Tobin

Nowhere is the elusive power of the economy more evident than in the foreign exchange trade. Every day, more than 1.5 trillion dollars are traded in the international financial markets. Less than five percent of that amount has to do with payments for goods or services. The rest is involved in speculative transactions among the now more than 180 negotiable currencies in the world. It's a business that keeps world economy in a state of constant destabilization. The foreign exchange trade regularly forces developing countries to undergo devaluations, with painful consequences for millions of poor people. But the West is afflicted by this speculation fever as well. In 1992, speculators compelled England to withdraw the pound from the European Monetary System (EMS). If the dollar rises, then oil (which is paid for in dollars) becomes more expensive, causing energy bills to rise. Et cetera. So politicians, and especially their independent representatives in this game – the presidents of the central banks – do everything they can to limit fluctuations in the exchange rates. More rest on the currency front means more rest in trade, which means more stability in the economy. That's why central bankers are so often in the news, trying to make "their" currency look as good as possible. That's also why they threaten to raise or lower the interest rate (or threaten not to) – in order to influence the appeal of their currency. Central banks also regularly buy massive amounts of currencies, to thereby support the exchange rate or to force it down.

All that effort has meager results. The influence exerted by central banks on the international money flow is no longer significant. Speculators are always beating out the central bankers. The euro drops, no matter what president Wim Duisenberg of the European Central Bank says or does. He's powerless in the face of the 1.5 trillion dollars that change hands every day. That rearguard action is strikingly illustrative of how the power of money has humanity in its grip. You can look with pity at Duisenberg and his colleagues, because in the end it's the entire world population – except for a few lucky speculators – who are the victims of the foreign exchange trade. The waste of energy on the currency front is all the more tragic because an instrument does exist that can effectively stand up to the enormous power of money. It's an instrument that can significantly strengthen the position of human individuals in the economy. It's a familiar instrument: taxation.

There is a tax plan that can help restrain harmful currency speculation. More about that later. Generally speaking, taxes can make important contributions on the road to a more humane economy, both through the way taxes are imposed and through the kind of taxes imposed. It may seem strange to present taxes as a solution to the imbalance in the modern economy. Many people regard the paying of taxes as a necessary evil and not as an instrument of renewal. Historically, taxation systems have always been on the wrong side. The history of taxes goes back to authoritarian regimes – to kings and other non-elected rulers – that needed money for wars. The ruler had the money collected from his subjects under threat of sword. So taxes were hated. They bred revolutions, which were conducted under mottoes such as "no taxation without representation." In most of the world, revolutions have actually solved this particular question. Today, the tax collector – or his boss at any rate – is an elected official. But what remains nevertheless is the feeling of arbitrariness. As far as that's concerned, the tax payer in democratic societies is no better off.

The taxation system still reflects something dictatorial; it's based on the interests of the state, not on the wishes of the citizens, the customers.

The relationship between tax revenues and the spending of those revenues certainly went astray after the introduction of the income tax about a century ago. You hand over a portion of your income to the tax authorities, but no one can tell you what part of that amount will be spent for what purpose. Taxes serve a good purpose – that's beyond doubt. No one disputes the necessity of schools, hospitals and roads. But it would make such a difference if you could ride past a new school and have the feeling that you had made a contribution to its construction. Sometimes such a relationship does exist. The "radio and TV contribution" is used to finance the public broadcasting companies, and the "removal contribution" that we pay when we buy a new car is used to recycle that car later on. The relationship is crystal clear and quite sensible. Is it accidental that in both cases it's literally the word *contribution* that is actually used? Isn't that the essence of the payment, and a much more pleasant word than "tax"?

A clear relationship between taxation and the spending of the revenues would stimulate the sense of involvement in society. You could tax the incomes of university graduates in order to finance universities, levy excise taxes on cigarettes to support health care – and not let all those excise taxes flow into one big pot that the government reaches into at its own discretion, which is what happens today.

Alvin Toffler, author of such books as *The Third Wave*, has made a simple proposal for stimulating involvement in the paying of taxes. Each tax form would contain a space where the most important tasks and functions of the government could be listed. The tax payer could then distribute one percent of his or her tax money among those categories. One person would put everything into education. Another would choose to improve the infrastructure and health care. This would produce a "citizens' budget," which would provide insight into the priorities of the population at large. It would be fascinating to compare that budget with the customary budget resulting from compromises among officials, politicians and lobbies. This citizens' budget would not threaten state financing. Parliament would decide on 99 percent of the tax revenues in the customary manner anyway. Undoubtedly the parliament would have good reasons for ignoring or honoring particular requests that emerge from the citizens' budget. But the basic idea is that the difference between the two budgets would spark a discussion that would give all the tax payers some insight into the way their money is being spent. That discussion would shift the accent from tax revenues and budgetary figures to human initiatives and needs.

Taxation can have an important guiding effect on the economy, and the current tax system is remarkably unsympathetic in that respect. The state collects most of the tax revenues via income taxes. Work is the main source of tax monies. Taxes make work expensive and therefore scarce. For a business it's quite simple: the more people you employ, the more tax money you pay. For this reason, each company tries to hire as few people as possible. The use of energy and raw materials, on the other hand, is barely taxed at all and is even directly or indirectly subsidized. In other words, the current tax regime stimulates unemployment and the wasteful use of energy and raw materials, two negative effects in one. This system leads, for instance, to the mindlessness of the glass recycling station. Fully intact bottles and pots are tossed in, ground to smithereens and sent to the oven to make exactly the same bottles and pots from the remains. The raw materials for glass are cheap, and so is the energy used to stoke the oven for the second, third or fourth time in order once again to make new glass from shards. But it's expensive to pay people to oversee the collection and re-use of the same bottles and pots.

Dutch entrepreneur Eckart Wintzen has proposed an alternative to the tax system that is meant to solve this abuse. He wants to tax the use of raw materials and energy and at the same time reduce the tax on labor. The idea is that a company would have to pay more to use more raw materials and energy than to put more people on the employment rolls. In this upside-down tax system, employment is stimulated and the environment is protected at the same time. This plan goes much further than the introduction of the eco-tax. The eco-tax is an energy duty on the use of oil, gas and coal. Wintzen wants a system that also taxes the use of other raw materials – woods and metals, for instance. A system like this is aimed at an economy in which service is central. A masseur who comes to your house every day is more attractive than buying a new bed. And obviously you'd prefer a non-gas-guzzling car that comes *with* a chauffeur. Companies would search for ways to distinguish themselves through the services they offer to go with their products. Repairs and perfect service would become more interesting than the high-speed development of a new generation of products. Disposable articles would be replaced by service products. A situation would arise in which the economic priorities of the business community would coincide with the long-term interests of both humanity and the planet.

The question, of course, is how much the use of raw materials and energy should be taxed. For the answer to that question, Wintzen introduces the notion of "extracted value." The new tax is called the value extracted tax, or VET – analogous to the VAT, or value added tax. The extracted value is the value that a certain product or raw material extracts from the environment through human use. By way of example: a car uses oxygen and produces carbon dioxide. The VET for the car owner is equal to the costs entailed in reversing that process – planting the number of trees necessary to turn all the carbon dioxide that the car has produced back into oxygen, for instance. The essence of the new tax is to reduce the environmental damage caused by a certain product to the level at which nature itself is capable of clearing up the remaining consequences. Sometimes materials are used that cannot be reclaimed (at least not in the near future), such as certain metals. In this case, the user would have to pay VET to cover the development of a sustainable alternative to these products.

Wintzen proposes a phased introduction of the VET over a period of about fifteen years, with a simultaneous reduction of the income tax, so production and services can gradually be adapted by the business community. The introduction of the VET guide steer wealthy Western countries – where work is often scarce and consumption levels are high – towards a more decent, cleaner economy. But when it comes to strengthening the position of human individuals in the world economy, there's much more to be done, particularly in the developing countries. A tax scheme developed by the American Nobel Prize winner James Tobin may be an answer to this challenge. In 1978, Tobin proposed the introduction of a tax on international financial transactions. The purpose of this plan was to discourage currency speculation. After the abandonment of the fixed rate of exchange in 1971 and the subsequent oil crisis, there followed a period of frequent unrest in the international exchange markets. Tobin's aim with his tax was to calm market fluctuations. He did not immediately give thought to how the revenues of the new tax would be spent. At first, Tobin received little support for his initiative. The governments of the principal industrial countries still viewed the system of floating exchange rates as mainly beneficial.

About ten years later, the "Tobin tax" received new attention.

First of all, the international currency market had grown enormously: from perhaps 100 billion dollars a day when James Tobin first made his proposal, to more than one trillion dollars a day. In the meantime, governments had finally been convinced of the harmful effects of currency speculation, and central banks did everything they could to limit those effects. When the pound dropped out of the EMS (the forerunner of the euro and the European Central Bank) in 1992, it was taken as a omen. The current international flows of capital are almost never used for financing world trade or foreign investment, but are mainly aimed at making money from the foreign exchange trade. The introduction of the "Tobin Tax" would limit speculation fever and give central banks more power over private investors. In addition, governments are looking for new forms of taxation in response to globalization. Multinational corporations spread out their activities in order to pay as little tax as possible. Multinationals focus their labor-intensive activities in countries where labor is cheap, and they make sure their profit is low in countries where taxes are high. This development is a challenge to the introduction of new taxes. The potentially gigantic revenues involved make the introduction of the Tobin Tax especially attractive. Those revenues also explain the interest of many development organizations that want to use the tax on foreign currency transactions to finance Third World development.

The rate of the Tobin Tax would be quite limited – between 0.1 and 0.5 percent of every transaction. This rate means that each time 100 euros or dollars are traded, 10 to 50 cents in taxes would be paid. A rate like this barely qualifies as a tax for normal trade and investments. Nevertheless, the low rate would have a profound effect on the short-term foreign currency trade. For someone dealing in currency every day, the tax would really mount up. At a rate of 0.5 percent, someone who conducts daily transactions valued at a million euros would pay 1.2 million euros a year in taxes (based on about 240 business days a year). For someone handling the same amount per week, the rate would drop to 260,000 euros a year, and the monthly dealer would pay only 60,000 euros a year. In other words, the biggest speculators pay the most. If you consider that 40 percent of all currency transactions have a time horizon of less than two days – and 80 percent have less than a week – it's clear that the Tobin Tax would have a calming effect on this area of trade. As a consequence, of course, revenues would decrease; the more successful the Tobin Tax is in combating currency speculation, the lower the tax yields would be. But even if current trading were to drop by half, a 0.2 percent Tobin Tax would still bring in about 300 billion dollars a year. The value of that amount is all the greater when you compare it with the 225 billion dollars the United Nations says it needs every year for dealing with the world's most severe poverty and environmental pollution.

The Tobin Tax restricts the amount of currency speculation undermining economic development and at the same time helps re-establish justice in the world. These are very attractive consequences from "throwing a bit of sand" in the machinery of the financial markets, as James Tobin himself says at the beginning of this chapter. The Canadian parliament recently supported initiatives to introduce the Tobin Tax, being the first representative body to pass a motion in which the government was called on "to demonstrate leadership and, in cooperation with the international community, to introduce a tax on financial transactions." Leadership indeed. New taxes could direct the development of the world economy towards greater respect for people and for the environment.

A corporation has no heart, no soul, no morals. It cannot feel pain.
— Kalle Lasn

6 GROUNDING THE CORPORATION

Pacific Lumber is an American family firm exploiting old sequoia forests in California. The company, set up by great-great-grandfather Murphy in the nineteenth century, acquired forests and felled trees for lumber. Due care was paid to reforestation, vital for the company's continuity. A small town sprang up. Employees were well paid and looked after, right down to their children being sent off to university by the company who also paid the fees. So far so good. Pacific Lumber was a capitalist success story. But then in the 1970s father Murphy, the Murphy now in charge, decided to realize part of the family assets by selling shares in the company on Wall Street. At first this had no effect on the way the firm was run, the family continuing as they always had. But in the mid-1980s buying mania broke out in Wall Street. All sorts of companies were bought by adventurers with enormous amounts of borrowed capital – junk bonds. Michael Milken and the Drexel Burnham Lambert Bank were the main players – they would later pay heavily for their role in the junk-bond saga – and these were the parties that enabled Texan investor Charles Hurwitz to make a hostile takeover bid. The president of the lumber company was woken at half past five in the morning by a call from Hurwitz announcing that he was at that very moment telling Wall Street of his plans. It was just like a scene from the movies. Taken completely by surprise, Pacific Lumber was unable to mount any serious resistance.

Hurwitz was heavily in debt, and the only way to pay it off

quickly was to turn the company's capital – forests containing trees up to 1,500 years old – into liquid assets. Pacific Lumber had been making about 25 million dollar profit a year; now at least 100 million dollar was necessary to service Hurwitz's debt. Scores of years of careful exploitation of the forests were sacrificed by Charles Hurwitz to raise the money he needed. Reforestation programs could not keep up with the rate at which trees were now being felled. This ecological terrorism found immediate opposition amongst environmental activists, culminating in 'a war between Wall Street and Main Street' as David Harrison grippingly describes it in his book The Last Stand. The issues of employment and the value of a natural resource were drowned in a flurry of dramatic demonstrations and court cases which continue to this day; one recent 'climax' being twenty-six-year-old Julia Hill who saved at least one sequoia from the axe by installing herself, 54 meters up in it, for two years.

Welcome to the stock market. The above tragedy is a direct result of this generator of affluence. Share prices over the past ten years have risen by more than 300 per cent on average. Masses of people have made their fortunes by playing the market. Even so, a price has to be paid for such an accumulation of capital. Money streams on to the stock markets, but the responsibility for company policy is spread thinly. In the case of Pacific Lumber, the damage is clear; in many other cases, less so. The price of market euphoria is evident, for instance, in the increased pressure in business on work and achievement. The share price must go up; so every quarterly result has to be higher than the preceding one. Share prices are followed, minute by minute. Shares change hands constantly. In 1960 only 10 per cent of the shares on Wall Street changed hands in a year. By 1990 that had already gone up to almost 50 per cent, and now more than three-quarters of shares change hands every year. Investors are impatient. They want profit, and quickly. The stock market has become a stress factor both for investors and businesses. Companies listed on the stock market barely get the chance to carry out any well thought-out long-term policy; wise policy would block short-term results. Is it any wonder that employees are falling victim to heart attacks at an ever younger age? Is it any wonder that businesses regularly cave in under the pressure and carry out activities that are both environmentally and socially damaging, and which will also, in the end, damage their own image? This is the reality behind the constantly rising share-price index.

The stock market is the symbol of the worthlessness of modern society. Values do not count, only money. This is what makes the comparison of the stock market with a casino so apt. The casino is very far removed from the original function of the stock market. At one time the stock market's function was to raise finance for investment in industry. The stock market made it possible for businesses to raise funds under more attractive conditions than those offered by the banks. Rather than having repeatedly to meet crushing interest payments to a bank, the company could pay shareholders a dividend of the profits made, at a convenient moment. In practice, this fine system rarely works. It does when there is a launch of a new company; then shareholders do indeed provide the capital needed for the company to start new activities. How often though has a launch been used to make a fortune for the original shareholders! The system also works when a newly listed company issues new shares to raise money for investment. But most trading on the stock market concerns trade in shares which have already passed from hand to hand many times. In such cases there is no question of any direct financing of a company. If I buy a share in Shell, the money doesn't go to Shell but to the person whose share I have bought. This sort of trading is primarily in the interests of the shareholder rather than in the interests of Shell. There is of course something to be said for someone – who years before lent capital to Shell – being able to sell his shares to another. By being able to trade freely in shares, a punter will be more inclined to invest in a company – and this is in Shell's interest. After all, you can get your money back when you need it. But if the result of the free market is that no relationship is left between the shareholder – who is formally a joint owner of the company – and the company, the situation is wide open to abuse.

Indicative of this is the use in stock-market reports nowadays of the word 'investors'. 'Shareholders' implies involvement in the company. The investor, on the other hand, is primarily concerned with his own interests. He invests his own money in the way most attractive to him, not bothering with the effect his trading might have on the company in which he is investing, just as long as his share price rises. The egocentric investor has turned the stock market into a casino of speculation and hostile takeovers. Funds listed on the market prey on each other, reckoning that the value of the competitor's property is higher than what is listed. These funds are bought with borrowed money and are then sold piecemeal for profit. Such activity pushes up the share prices. Takeovers financed mainly by borrowed capital are at odds with greater considerations, those of man and nature in the economy. Loans have to be redeemed and interest has to be paid on them. In order to do this, companies have to maximize profits and step up production, often with negative consequences such as increased pollution and redundancies. In other words, on the road to greater riches, companies listed on the stock market are virtually forced to damage society.

Companies are getting bigger and bigger and more and more powerful. Companies set processes in motion that can affect future generations. Pharmaceutical companies, as they strive for growth, profit and a higher share price, can introduce products on the market which will still be taking their toll a hundred years later. Tankers containing oil or chemicals can ravage the environment for scores of years. Nuclear power stations and chemical plants are sited near cities. The list of accidents waiting to happen is long, the responsibilities correspondingly high. But who takes responsibility? Who is responsible for the crazy policy of Pacific Lumber? There is a great responsibility gap in the economy. When a company causes damage, virtually nothing happens. It may be required to pay a fine, a huge one. It may face a consumer boycott. Shareholders may suffer a fall in share price and sell their shares as a result. In theory, directors and commissioners can nowadays be prosecuted for irresponsible policies; in fact, they rarely are. Usually when there is a débâcle the top director simply moves on to another company. Society, the public, is left with the damage and the company simply continues its activities under new leadership. Isn't it odd that the shareholders – who own a company – are not jointly responsible for that company's policy? Shouldn't investing money carry responsibilities with it? Or does a share only give a right to a dividend? If a company does well the shareholder in the stock-market casino can recoup his stake many times, but when that company causes damage to society, the worst that can happen to the shareholder is that he loses his stake. Isn't this unbalanced, given the great influence the commercial world has on society?

Shareholders often complain of their lack of power. In the Netherlands all sorts of legal provisions stand in the way of the shareholder exercising any influence on company policy. In the Netherlands, a negligent management cannot be forced by the shareholders to resign. Investors are convinced that this situation has a dampening effect on share prices and they would like more influence – more rights – in the hope that this will increase the value of their shares. But are they also prepared to take more responsibility?

The lack of any responsibility on the part of the shareholder of a corporation is historical. It's a construction that was thought up in the Netherlands. The archetype of the corporation was the United East India Company of 1602 (Verenigde Oost-Indische Compagnie: VOC). Before the VOC, company debts – responsibilities – were carried over from generation to generation. Limited liability came into being with the discovery of the new world. The initiative to carry spices from Asia in wooden sailing vessels was not without heavy risk. Hence limited liability: a financier could never lose more than his investment. The state could assign a company this new form. Originally this was the result of negotiations where it was also agreed, for instance, that the state would enjoy part of the profit from the business. So originally, limited liability was granted as a favour by the state under certain conditions. The authorities granted permission to businesses to operate in this way. This brilliant discovery encouraged risk-taking and gave an enormous boost to overseas trade in the seventeenth century. Limited liability was not a privilege to be taken for granted. In time, this changed to the present situation where anyone may set up an Inc. or a plc for a fixed sum of money. There is no longer any question of individual negotiation with the authorities for a quid pro quo. No one now reckons that he's being issued with a right when he sets up his Inc.

Businessmen and their legal advisers four centuries ago expected to incur large debts that they could not pay off; this was the worst drawback they faced – if we don't count their 'plundering' of the new world – for which they sought protection. Nowadays many other factors – the environment, public health – are involved. No one then expected the present situation where business has potentially become one of the most dangerous forms of human activity. In the days of the VOC, there was no question of factories causing people to die through negligent production procedures; nor were there companies whose waste contained poisonous substances that would be released and end up in the food chain. In other words: circumstances have changed radically yet the legal form has stayed the same as in the seventeenth century. In fact it has even become easier for business: VOC directors had to negotiate with the state about limiting their liabilities; the modern entrepreneur simply heads for the Chamber of Commerce and fills in a form. Through this automatic process, the company has become more than a group of people developing some given activity; it has become a sort of 'social technology' with a life of its own. A company can continue after its founders die. Directors come and go, as do employees. The assets of a company can, through the stock market, become diffuse and broadly based. Shares in a company can be sold. Companies can merge. Despite all these changes the company 'lives' on as long as enough money is earned to pay for the expenses. But this independent company has no soul and feels no pain. When a company damages someone or something, it cannot show regret and say sorry. The anomaly is that a company has the rights of a human being with none of the obligations.

Big business fiercely resists any suggestion of more control. Companies complain constantly that they're already weighed down by rules and regulations. Perhaps what should be asked is: why are there so many rules? Perhaps what regulation does exist is the result of companies gradually becoming too influential in society, too undemocratic, and with only one official goal: to make profit. The reality of the modern company cries out for legal liability rules to be adapted. Things can no longer stay as they are, with a company – a group of people – having less responsibility than the individuals who make it up. The broad social gains derived from business in VOC days were obvious in a way that is no longer the case. This altered reality demands another legal structure. Two changes immediately spring to mind. Firstly, the privilege of setting up a company with limited liability should be retractable. In fact, a formal legal stipulation that a company can be dissolved when general interests are damaged does exist, but in practice it is ignored, even after great scandals. It is curious that the individual who breaks the law can end up in prison while the company which flouts it may be liable to a fine – often, paradoxically, tax-deductible – while remaining 'free'. It must become simpler and more natural for the community to close down a company when it flouts rules and gravely damages society. Some forfeit their right of existence and deserve to be closed down. How long may companies go on polluting, dumping and damaging before they are closed down and their assets sold in order, for instance, to pay damages to the community? When a firm continually abuses or violates public trust, then citizens should have the right to withdraw its right to trade and effectively close it down.

Even more can be done to curb companies. How would the world of the stock market seem if shareholders were again made personally liable for the policy of the company which, after all, they partly own? Removing limited liability would be a drastic but effective step in the right direction to a more human economy. Shareholders would then invest their money carefully on the stock market. They would pay close attention not just to a business' profit potential, but also to the manner in which it operates. They would choose companies who serve people and the natural world well. Removing limited liability would force shareholders to take responsibility for the activities of their companies. People would again become responsible for people. The stock market would stop being a casino. But who – critics might ask – would then still dare to make necessary large-scale investments with their corresponding high risks? Indeed. Yet has the experience of the past century not taught us that operating on such a large scale is a virtual guarantee of unwanted side-effects and abuses? In other words, once a company becomes too big for human responsibility, it is liable to cause inhuman damage. No matter how much we owe to the brilliant discovery of the VOC, this is what it has led to. In the end, it is only reasonable that companies should observe the same moral laws as we do as individuals.

Changes in corporation law will return business to the public domain and will help destroy that curious difference between work and home, since fathers – and it is still primarily fathers – behave in business in a way that they would not dream of behaving with their families at home. At the office they run an advertising campaign to stimulate the consumption of coffee among children – to contribute to turnover, of course, and a rise in the share price – and then they come home and tell their own children not to drink too much coffee; it's bad for them. Companies led by parents treat nature completely differently than they do their own gardens. Businessmen and women do things outside the home that they would not dream of doing at home. Companies should be treated as people. Not differently.

The medical establishment has become a major threat to health.
– Ivan Illich

7 THE EASIEST WAY

Human beings are good at making themselves peripheral. We ourselves have chosen the system of money-with-interest that has landed us in an exhausting debt race. And the tax system undermining our environment wasn't imposed on us by extraterrestrials either. Nor is the trading fever currently threatening our communities any less our own doing. One by one, they're all conscious choices for which we're now facing the consequences. Naturally, they weren't all choices made with the best intentions, and it's always easy to be right in retrospect, but there's a remarkable thread running through these decisions by which we organize our world: we always go for what's big and far away, we go for size. We keep allowing ourselves to be seduced by the path of technology and immensity, and we go on to lose our way in our own creation. We make systems and organizations in which people no longer count. It's as if we have consistently decided not to take the route that's easiest and closest to home. This tendency was apparent in the previous chapters dealing with the basic principles of our economic policy. It is a tendency that you're constantly bumping into in daily life – in the hospital, for instance, or in the supermarket, or in dealings with the power company. This chapter takes these three examples as a point of departure and shows how we ourselves can enhance the humanity in our environment by making new choices – how you yourself can contribute to a world where people count.

Take health care. Modern medicine is one of the triumphs of the twentieth century. Most people are convinced that a family member or friend would have died without a certain pill or intervention by the doctor, that we owe our health to technology. But the fact that we live twice as long today as people did a century ago is not owing to expensive medical technology and huge hospitals. Cholera, typhoid fever, tuberculosis and dysentery were on the wane before the arrival of antibiotics and vaccinations. The cause: hygiene and better food. Granted, the importance of these factors was first discovered and announced by doctors, but soap and boiled water are not medicine. It's typical that the man who performed the world's first heart transplant, the South African doctor Christiaan Bernard, pointed to Thomas Crapper as one of humanity's greatest benefactors. Crapper was an English plumber who invented the flush toilet. The great progress in modern medicine in this century has to do with "emergency aid." If you're struck by an acute, life-threatening infection, a heart attack, a serious traffic accident or an operable tumor, you can't do better than a Western hospital. But most of our complaints by far are chronic disorders, cancer, heart and vascular diseases. And as far as they're concerned, Western health care has lamentably little to offer. Ancient plagues have been replaced by new ones. At the same time, the costs of medical care have increased to such an extent that politicians are anxiously wondering whether it will all be affordable later on.

The core of the problem is the outlook of modern health care: health is the normal human state, and illness is an external influence, an enemy that must be fought. Health care often closely resembles a military operation. Even the terminology is the same: the *war* against cancer.... Doctors see the body as a machine in which faulty parts can be replaced. That machine can be run from the outside by means of medicines and medical technology. The commercial implications are immense, and advertising makes sure the patient really believes in the equation "more money + more medicine = more health." Within this industrial care system the patient is defenseless; procedures count more than people – it's inherent in the system. Wherever technology reigns, autonomy is lost. And that loss is the first step on the road to disease.

Healing cannot be regarded as an industry. Healing is a complex process in which – contradictory to the current Western perception – many factors play a role, not only medicines and tangible cells, but also intangible things such as hope, faith, trust, friendship, attention and will power. This is how prayer heals. Doctors know from experience that the patient who asks "why" when blood samples are taken, and who won't get undressed without an explanation, is usually better off. And what's going on when a mother begins producing antibodies in her milk for her baby suffering from an infection? All doctors take the oath of Hippocrates, but do they realize – they who are constantly interfering with the natural processes of the body – that the old Greek master once said, "the natural healing power within us is the most important power for recovery"? That's why the medicine of the Chinese, Indians and American Indians and other "primitive peoples" is aimed at supporting the body's own self-healing processes. Those traditions are based on the idea that nature is perfect and that the body wants to be healthy.

More and more frequently we hear stories about people who are mysteriously healed of incurable diseases – people, for instance, who are dismissed as hopeless cases because the doctors can no longer treat their tumors. They walk out of the hospital – and out of the system of health care – choose their own way, and are "miraculously" healed. Years later, the scans show no sign of a tumor. Modern medicine dismisses these kinds of cases as "anecdotal" because there's no concrete explanation for them. But perhaps these anecdotes are proof of the self-healing capabilities of the body? Perhaps the main purpose of treatment and medicine should be to stimulate the spontaneous healing process already in the body?

One phenomenon that is just as old as medicine itself seems to point in that direction. It is known that people become better after taking remedies that trigger no demonstrable physical results: the *placebo* effect, Latin for "I will please." It is easy to accept the claim that the therapeutic effect of the medicines and concoctions made by doctors of the past can be traced to the placebo effect. Those preparations had no demonstrable medicinal results. But the same applies to most modern medicines. Scientific effects have been established for only twenty percent of all modern medications. This means that doctors are prescribing pills and treatments that are essentially inert. But that doesn't mean they don't work. Their healing power comes from the placebo effect. Placebos have been shown to provide significant relief to seventy percent of patients for many disorders – from pain to high blood pressure and rheumatoid arthritis. Placebos are even effective against psychiatric disorders – depression. In any case, they're no less effective than "real" medications.

The simple fact that the doctor prescribes a pill is evidently enough to promote healing. Here expectation and trust play a decisive role, that trust grows in proportion to the attention provided by the doctor. Several placebo studies show that the doctor himself or herself is the best medicine. A doctor who listens, mobilizes the patient's self-healing capacities. The placebo effect also shows that all forms of "medicine" are effective as long as the patient believes in them. This explains the increasing success of alternative medicine. Aside from the fact that methods of treatment such as homeopathy and acupuncture have exhibited a wide range of proven medicinal effects, alternative medicine in general shows much more respect for the patient. It involves an integral approach instead of an attack on symptoms. Alternative doctors usually give their patients much more time and attention. They listen to the whole story, including feelings of despair and grief. That attention restores the patient's "belief" in his own healing process.

Attention and care – the human being – are therefore crucial factors in health care. But in the "expensive" modern health care system there's hardly any room for the human being with these "cheap" qualities. The doctor who tries to pay attention to his patients is badgered by hospital directors and insurance companies calling for "efficiency." We're talking not only about the human being known as the "doctor," but also about family and friends. Human relations are of vital importance for health. It has been found that most people who die of a heart attack actually die of loneliness. Studies have also shown that women with breast cancer who participate in weekly conversation groups with fellow patients stay alive twice as long on the average as women who do not. In Western society, care has been organized and institutionalized and the result is increasing loneliness. Neighborliness saves more lives than an ambulance. Indeed, the siren of an ambulance pushes humanity to the side; it's not my problem, it's a problem of the system. More humanity involved in health care means more health, less dependence on technology and expensive medicine and therefore lower costs. Remember the American health insurance company that offered a discount to people who participated in a Lets group (chapter 2). The system that focuses on the human being, and in which technology plays a supportive role, is a better, more effective system, but it's not the system we've chosen. The good news, however, is that everyone, at every moment of their lives, can decide to take the easiest path to health.

Food production is another important area in which human beings have been pushed aside – with disastrous results. We often hear today that biotechnology is needed to feed humanity. The same thing was said thirty years ago concerning chemical fertilizers and pesticides. But the claim that only large-scale, chemical – that is, inhuman – agriculture can produce sufficient food for the rapidly growing masses in developing countries is a lie. It is not true that keeping pigs in multi-tiered flats is an unavoidable next step in food production. The solution to the food problem is not biotechnology. That solution must start with a critical look at the food trade. Developing countries are forced to produce food for export by the IMF and the World Bank. Farmers in Chile, Mexico and Africa produce apples and pears for the European and American market when these fruits are out of season in the northern hemisphere. And most of the food that developing countries cultivate for themselves is regarded as fodder in the West. Export production takes the place of local food production. Because of this, Chileans, Mexicans and Africans must keep buying their own food – if they have enough money – from Western multinational corporations that import food to their countries. Free trade also stimulates monoculture. Many inhabitants of the earth eat wheat today, even though up until recently they didn't know what wheat was. Imagine what it would be like if you could no longer obtain meant, only soybeans – thanks to free trade. This one-sidedness also occurs in production. Only a few decades ago, Indian farmers cultivated thousands of varieties of rice; today that's a few dozen at the most. But there was a good reason for all those varieties. Not every variety of grain grows with the same success in every part of the world. The rye that grows in northern France can be very vulnerable in Argentina. And that explains why in Brazil, for example, up until five years ago there were an average of twenty new agricultural sicknesses or plagues a year, while today there are more than 300. Indoctrinated by the alleged successes of the Green Revolution, Brazilian farmers usually solve the growing problem by using more pesticides.

And that is a dead end street, as their Indian colleagues are learning in increasing numbers. Around thirty years ago, after the successes of the sixties, the Green Revolution ran aground in India. The intensive irrigation had caused the groundwater level to drop dramatically, and vermin had become resistant to the excessive amounts of pesticides and chemical fertilizers. For many crops, the yield per hectare has dropped. The problem is that Indian farmers, aided by irrigation, chemical fertilizers and pesticides, have begun raising crops that do not thrive in that environment. So a counter movement is now taking shape: farmers are starting to plant native crops once again, using natural, organic pesticides such as an extract from the native neem tree, which effectively protects cotton plants. The yield per acre is rising again ... and farmers are producing for the local market once more.

The use of chemical pesticides is not only harmful for nature, but for human beings as well – at least for farmers. It is well known that banana and coffee farmers are suffering terribly because of the large-scale spraying of trees and plants on their land. And we still haven't mentioned the ultimate effect of these agents on the health of the consumer. It's hard to call industrial agriculture a human success. The return to native, organic agriculture today is a world-wide phenomenon. From Honduras and Senegal to the Philippines, striking successes are being achieved by switching over to the organic production of native crops, with fifty- to one-hundred-percent improvements in harvests being reported. But even when there is no apparent increase in the direct yield of a crop, the switch results in more food. Because when the use of chemical pesticides is halted, auxiliary yields begin reappearing on or near the fields such as snails, fish and birds. In addition, farmers stop focusing on one crop alone, which had usually been a grain. Combinations of crops appear to yield more. A field that is planted in corn (maize) alone all year long yields less than a field sown with a combination of crops, such as corn, beans and pumpkins. Studies have now shown that it would be quite possible to feed the population of the world without poison and chemical fertilizer.

The fact that poison is poisonous, and that it can be harmful to human health via plants, will be proven once again. But more important is the fact that organic farming restores the relationship between human beings and nature, and between human beings and animals, and among human beings themselves – because native, organic farming is far more rooted in the community. Those who choose organic food are not only deciding in favor of their own health, but are contributing to a system of food production in which people count as well.

Energy is the third area in which humans have made choices that end up being bad for them. Smoking chimneys, exhaust gasses, smog, the greenhouse effect – more and more, the fossil fuel economy is undermining our environment. But a more compassionate energy revolution is underway. While environmental organizations send representatives to climate conferences to lobby politicians, who don't dare take any big steps forward, private institutes and small companies are discovering the path to an economy that's solar-powered. It's a development that to a significant extent is withdrawing from the realm of states and governments. The power station of the future will not be supervised by the World Bank or the European Commission, but will be a solar cell on the roof or a windmill in the garden. Later on, energy will be literally homemade. Those who think that the energy industry today is still the mightiest sector in the global society might try imagining what kinds of fundamental changes the development of a sustainable economy would mean. Relinquishing influence is not a popular choice. The resistance of the oil industry and the established energy companies is still considerable, but human individuals are unmistakably making their own way back to the sun.

Up until the Industrial Revolution, every person was totally dependent on the sun. The sun provided warmth, provided the wood used to kindle fire and caused the growth of food. Industrialization broke the link between humans and their source of life. From then on, energy was something you dug out of the ground. And since no one could do that alone, powerful organizations were developed. Coal, oil and gas opened up tremendous new possibilities. Yet the detour inherent in this choice of fossil fuels is striking. An automobile is barely one percent efficient. For every hundred liters of fuel it consumes, only one liter is actually involved in the moving of passengers. And less than ten percent of the energy needed to heat the filament of a lamp is transformed into visible light. The efficiency of washing machines and dish washers, refrigerators, dryers and other household appliances can be improved on short notice by a factor of ten. The same is true for energy consumption in office buildings.

The development of better and more efficient products can be greatly stimulated by switching from fossil fuels to sustainable sources of energy, because these fuels require lighter products. The car of the future will be able to ride a hundred kilometers on one liter of fuel, and that fuel – in the form of hydrogen, whose only "exhaust fume" would be water – will be generated on board with solar cells. A car like that is a power plant on wheels. Such breakthroughs begin at the beginning: with the sun. Every year, the sun produces 2.5 million exajoules of energy on earth. That amount of energy is more than 7000 times the world's total annual energy consumption. In other words, the total amount of fossil fuels that were available when the Industrial Revolution began was just as large as the amount of energy produced by thirty days of sunshine. That accounts for the detour.

The greatest contribution to the new energy revolution will come from solar cells, or the photovoltaic systems. PV systems turn sunlight directly into electricity. What's so promising about the solar cell is that it's made of silicon, which is the most common element on earth after oxygen. Twenty-eight percent of the earth's surface consists of silicon. PV cells have barely entered into mass production, which is why solar energy is still much more expensive than other sources of energy. Solar cells are made from the refuse produced in factories that manufacture computer chips – also made from silicon. That parallel sheds some light on the possibilities inherent in the solar cell. Every eighteen months for the past twenty years, the semiconductor industry has succeeded in doubling the amount of information that can be stored on a silicon chip. An exerted effort in solar cell production could result in an enormous breakthrough. The electronics revolution of the last century serves as an example. That motto of that development was different, faster, smaller, cheaper, more efficient and better. Energy production today is on the eve of the same kind of trend, and many enterprising pioneers are just itching to take over the world.

In any case, the public utility of the future will look quite different. Much more energy will be generated locally, such as at home on your roof with a PV system, or with a windmill out in the fields. Decentralized energy supply would mean the end of the big power plant. Small modular plants would be like cars compared with cathedrals. If more energy is needed, a PV system or a windmill could easily be added, and no gigantic, time-consuming investments would be necessary. Energy would become a regional matter. The generation of energy, and the jobs – and authority – needed to do it would remain close to home and would no longer be "imported" from outside – another way that the energy revolution would contribute to a more humane society.

Whether it's health care, food or energy, we're seeing the same tendency take shape in each case. People have let themselves be tempted by "green revolutions" and have ended up being duped. Major progress – more health, more food, more energy – has its flip side as well. Hospitals make patients feel defenseless. Large-scale agriculture depletes and exhausts the land. Generating energy suffocates and pollutes society. But the hopeful conclusion is that things could get better if we choose human solutions and systems that are closer to home – if we choose the easiest way. Because wherever technology and industry exceed human dimensions, problems arise.

How thin can I spread myself before I'm no longer "there"?
– John Perry Barlow

8 YOUR WORK OR YOUR LIFE

Our own work is our most important contribution to the economy. The way we do our work determines the place we set aside for ourselves – for the human individual – in the economy. And there's plenty of room for improvement as far as that's concerned. Just you look around and you get the impression that people don't matter very much in modern society.

A friend of mine works for a large bank. In the evening, when she wants to go home to her two children, she takes a stack of paper from her desk – "copy work" – and sneaks out the door, one of the first of her colleagues to do so. In the newspaper I read about the young lawyer, an employee at one of the big law offices, who wanted to work four days a week. His free choice was respected, but he had to forget any hopes of ever becoming a partner. That path was only open to those working a minimum of 1500 declarable hours a year. (This means something like seven declarable hours per workday, and requires long workdays with no room for anything else.) Another friend with an upper level marketing job at a large food concern moved with her husband and children to the other side of the world – Australia –in the hope of finding a society where there was room for more than work. And Robert Reich, President Clinton's Secretary of Labor, decided against renewing his term of office after he had called home once again to say he wouldn't be back that evening, and his nine-year-old son had asked, "Can you wake me up when you come home? I just want to know you're home."

Secretary of Labor? Secretary of Slavery is more like it. There's a new kind of slavery raging in our society, a slavery of death. The top-ranking official of one of the Netherlands' largest banks – a man in his sixties – made the despairing comment that he's losing more and more employees to heart attacks at the age of 45. The Japanese even have a word for it – *karoshi* – which means "death by overwork." The banker sees no solution. Yes, the main office has its own in-house physician, there are plenty of opportunities to take a paid leave of absence, and there's always the annual Christmas speech to provide a moment of reflection. But on the other 364 days competition reigns supreme. We're losing our lives as fast as we work to keep them.

Although the concept "reduction of working hours" has only recently been given a place in the Dutch lexicon, a recent survey conducted by the Congress of Dutch Trade Unions has determined that for almost half the Dutch workforce, overwork is the biggest problem. Obviously this phenomenon does not concern all employees, but its effect is most drastic on working parents and their children. I remember when I was young that my father was always home by half past six. He was away perhaps one evening a week, and occasionally he went on business trips. And my father was not unique. The fathers of my friends (only a few mothers worked at that time) were also usually home at night. My father also never talked about his "free time." He was just home. The concept of "free time" turns work into "unfree time" – prison. The historians of the future will have a tough time explaining why the enormous increase in prosperity that began back then was accompanied by parents having less and less time to raise their own children. At the beginning of the last century, a child didn't start school until age seven. Now it's no longer exceptional for a child of three months to be taken to a daycare center. Families go on vacation several times a year to increasingly exotic places, two cars per household is no longer unusual, houses are teeming with modern, electronic appliances, but there's no time for the children. In *Brave New World*, Aldous Huxley once drew a portrait of a nightmare society without families, where everyone was raised within a system of daycare centers. It's a bad dream that is busily becoming reality.

A daycare generation is now growing up at high speed without the sociologists of this research-addicted modern society having been able to determine what the consequences would be for the growth of children and for family ties. But you don't have to be a sociologist to get the feeling that children prefer to be with their parents – parents, not mothers. Always. Lack of attention, of emotional bonding at an early age, has a negative effect on the development of a self-image. So we're working on a harmful experiment by which many small, vulnerable souls will be brought into the world. Every day we're cooperating with an economy in which people don't count. The remedy, born of necessity, is called "quality time": it doesn't really matter how much time parents and children spend with each other as long as they make the most of it. In practice this mainly means going out for ice cream; parents and children have to have a "good time" when they're together. But it's not that simple. It's the difficult moments in relationships that form character, after all. You can't limit a relationship to good quality time. The fascinating study by the Austrian psychologist Bruno Bettelheim on the kibbutzim in Israel illustrates this. In the ideal kibbutz, children were raised collectively and contact with their parents was restricted to pleasant moments together. Bettelheim found that these children were strongly oriented towards their environment but had trouble making autonomous choices in society – between right and wrong, good and evil. Their "consciences" proved to be underdeveloped. And it is just that development that is essential for the growth of responsible citizens in a free society.

Parents would like things to be different. They'd like to be with their children, too. This partly explains the huge success of the web site *Watch Me!* (www.watch-me.com) in the United States. This site makes it possible for parents working in offices to see how it's going with their children or whether they're awake from their afternoon nap by means of cameras posted in daycare centers. It's a nice invention, but a visit to the site leaves you with an odd feeling about progress. A recent British study shows that in management circles the four-day workweek is "a suppressed ideal." Those with attractive positions are paid high salaries, but they're also forced to pay a high price. A reporter wrote a story about the commute he made every weekday by intercity train at six in the morning from Sittard to The Hague – and he could just as well have been taking the subway in London, Tokyo or New York: "Walk down the aisle and you see them lying, hanging: the slaves who've bartered away their sleep for filthy lucre." It's a full train that brings these commuters back again at nine o'clock at night. It's a cliché, of course, but nobody lies on his deathbed wishing he had spent more time at the office. So why do people choose these kinds of jobs, anyway?

Such slave trains – and daycare centers, too – are solutions to an identity crisis that are doomed to failure. You are what you do in this world, so you don't do just anything at all. In the past, your identity was determined by your village, church and parentage. If your father was a Catholic violin maker, that's what you became, too. And if your mother was a Protestant peasant, you would have the same future to look forward to. The Industrial Revolution liberated modern man and offered him something new: choice. An individual today can choose his own identity. Unfortunately, we haven't gotten any further than doing things. "Being" is not a form of identity for most people. That one-sidedness pushes humanity out of the economy and has also resulted in a new inferior class: parents. Parenthood, after all – despite the work of washing diapers, making sandwiches, and getting children to school on time – is "being" at its very best.

If work determines your identity, that explains why people (and this still applies more to men than to women) find it difficult to work less, why they don't just fight for their secret wish of a four-day workweek. Work gives life meaning, and that's why the prescription for the overworked society cannot simply read "work less." Yet more life begins with less work. And that's possible, even in this time of merciless competition. Europeans have an average vacation of six weeks, Americans two. Yet European businesses seem to be able to compete successfully with American companies. So working less does not mean that a company is any less effective. A great deal of time is needlessly lost in many organizations. Many people react with grim determination to problems that they encounter over and over again in their work. That grimness is a time-guzzler. It sounds strange, but the most effective way to solve these problems is this: lean back, relax, put your feet on your desk and take a break. Another ideal way to save time is to agree that meetings at the office will take place only before ten o'clock and after four o'clock. Many different organizations have shown fantastic results by following this simple rule.

"Saying no" to yet another meeting or gathering can be a valuable investment – not only in yourself but also in your company. It means that in just a moment your company can profit from a really fresh, creative employee. For the past few years, the personnel at the American 3M company – known for their little yellow sticky notes – have been expected to spend 15 percent of their working time fooling around. According to the 3M vision, fooling around promotes creativity. And wouldn't you know it, 30 percent of the 50,000 products that the company now makes were developed during the past four years. Internet guru John Perry Barlow once wrote this famous line as lyricist for *The Grateful Dead*: "Too much of everything is just enough." "It sounded good when I wrote it twenty years ago, but I don't believe it anymore: too much of everything is too much. I've realised that I must find the discipline to say 'no' more often. It sounds easy but it's not. Just when I have convinced myself that what I have is more than plenty, the phone rings, and someone offers me something that I can't refuse. But then I ask myself an important question: 'How thin can I spread myself before I am no longer there?'"

That squeezed feeling – familiar to so many – is partly caused by the strict division that arose this century between work and home. This division is an unfortunate product of the Industrial Revolution. Before the Revolution took place there was hardly any division between work and home, both on the farm and in the village. Indeed, work and home life weren't divided at all. And they still aren't divided in a great many parts of the world. Campaigners are ready to throw themselves into the breach to fight child labor, but a vast majority of the working children in developing countries work alongside their parents in the countryside or doing housework. This is not an attempt to idealize that life, which is often a hard struggle for survival, but as far as a humane existence is concerned, that simple rural existence scores at least no lower than our modern economy. Child labor isn't the problem. Working, living and learning can easily go hand in hand. Exploitation and "abuse" are the evils that must be combated – and not only in India or Nigeria but also in the office complexes at the outskirts of the modern city.

It's instructive that many tribal cultures have no word for "work." The ugly English word "job," which also has made its appearance in the Netherlands, originally meant an unpleasant chore. In modern society, you're privileged if you can look down from an upper floor of your mirror-walled office building and see your own house. And from the other way around, those who are at home regard office buildings as remote, inaccessible places. The promise that technology would bring work and home closer together has produced very little so far. For the moment, faxes, mobile telephones and e-mail have mainly required *more* work, even at home. Work is encroaching on private life without technology making more room for private life in the midst of work. Technology is turning people into mobile offices, making them wonder whether they will ever be home.

Coming home is difficult enough as it is because it's a matter of two worlds colliding: the world of competition and egoism, of taking and profits, colliding with the world of relationships and love, of giving and self-sacrifice. That's a painful conflict for which there is only one way out: different work. Work isn't just about daily bread; it's also about the daily search for meaning. The biggest taboo, therefore, is restoring work to the realm of love. Hordes of people spend each day doing work that has not taken possession of their hearts, producing cars and soft drinks cans of which there are already too many, preparing for mergers that may result in higher share prices but not in happier people, manufacturing products that are not at all healthy.

Perhaps it's time to stop beating around the bush and start being honest with ourselves. How long will we continue with this soulless way of working and producing things? The priest Matthew Fox, author of *The Reinvention of Work* (HarperCollins, 1994), preached a sermon a few years ago in a city in the American state of Michigan the day after an automobile manufacturing plant had been closed. "First of all," he said, "I'd like to express my sympathy with all those who have been affected by this closing. We'll all have to stand together to create some kind of social safety net. But I also want to say something else today. Maybe there's more going on here than a group of people losing their incomes. Maybe we all have to ask ourselves whether we really need more cars. There are already hundreds of millions of cars that are causing many of the problems we have on our planet. Of course you can say, we've always manufactured cars here. But if we think deeper, we have to ask ourselves what kind of work Mother Earth is asking of our generation. And what kind of work future generations are asking of us. To be honest, I don't think that it's making more cars."

It takes courage to get involved in such a confrontation. Most of all, it takes the conviction that each person has his own unique contribution to make, that no one has to take the job meant for someone else. The word "profession" can be traced to a concept that is perhaps lofty but is nonetheless apt: vocation, calling. If we would really listen to our inner calling, how many of us would make cars or cola cans? Who among us would spend long days in an office doing nothing but watching share prices go up? When our profession – literally our public declaration of who we are and what we stand for – coincides with our inner calling, we end up doing what is good for ourselves, for our children and for society at large. If your work is your vocation, passion and love begin flowing of their own accord. Parenthood is service to a new generation, and the same should apply to every kind of work. Once upon a time, work was "survival" – there was no choice. But now we have the choice – and the opportunity – to add something. If what we add is valuable, it will enrich our own lives and will free us from the shackles of stress that have entrapped us. Such work is not to be separated from life, because it is a lifework – not work for statues or history books, but work that fills and inspires our lives. And the strange thing is that as you continue living, you no longer focus on the number of hours that you "work." It's a small but essential step, from work as performance to work as service, from work for me to work for us. That's the kind of work that contributes to a human economy. That work is your life.

We are explorers, and the most compelling frontier of our time is human consciousness.

    – Edgar Mitchell, Apollo 14 crew member

9 THE REVENGE OF THE SPIRIT

I often go to France for my summer vacations, to a wide open area where there's hardly any artificial light at night. And almost every evening I'm confronted with my own existence. Sometimes I lie on my back and look up at the overwhelmingly starry sky. I look at the stars that provided the atoms of which I am made.

No stars, no me.

I look at the starlight that set off on its journey millions of years ago. The star I'm seeing now may have ceased existing a very long time ago. It's a spectacle that my consciousness cannot take in. The Big Bang theory tells me that the universe arose out of one primal explosion of energy. But when I look up at the clear traces of the Milky Way, the endlessness leaves me at a loss. *What* am I looking at? And what's it all for?

For me, the point of our existence lies hidden in that endless starry sky. Under those stars, I realize that economic growth – the amassing and dealing in more and more material goods – does not provide an answer to our deepest questions about life. The universe challenges our consciousness. That consciousness is what makes man unique in the history of evolution, but we only use 10 percent, maybe 15 percent of it. In the remaining 85 or 90 percent lie the answers and explanations to the questions that humanity has not been able to answer, despite all our material progress. If we so choose, we are standing on the threshold of a period of spiritual growth that will put our material existence in a whole new light.

It is well known that astronauts – the members of our species who have been closest to the endlessness of space – underwent mind-expanding experiences. You probably know about the effect of air travel and the view of human achievement from above the cloud cover. The first time it happens, it's quite extraordinary to look down from the air at everything that looms so large and problematic in daily life and to see it as trivial. But that experience is nothing compared with what the astronauts underwent when they looked at the earth – their planet – from space and saw it as a blue ball. It isn't surprising that one of the crew members of the Apollo 14, Edgar Mitchell, set up an institute in the United States in 1973 for deepening the development of consciousness. Because for Mitchell, as the sixth visitor to the moon, *that* was strikingly clear: the universe raises deep questions about the human spirit.

We don't know much about the future. Our visions of the future are projections. And the problem with those projections is that they're usually strongly influenced by what exists now. If today's society is marked by a combination of technology, communication and market economy, then the usual picture of the 21st century is more of the same: *more* technology, *more* communication and *more* market. On top of that, speed becomes *more* speed. So the future is mainly an accelerated version of the present.

But this vision of the future does not take the mystery of consciousness into account. In past centuries, man has enthusiastically pursued the discovery of everything that can be seen and touched. The overwhelming question regarding the "why" of existence is shoved aside for the sake of convenience. Democracy, technology and the market economy offer no answer to that question, but that doesn't mean evolution can escape it. In the words of the celebrated physicist Stephen Hawking, speaking from his wheelchair through a talking computer: "I don't believe the science fiction like *Star Trek* where people are essentially the same

400 years in the future." This remark concerns almost all science fiction. Over and over we see the focus placed on unbelievable technological discoveries in a world devoid of any new social breakthroughs. Hawking, on the other hand, predicts that biological systems will continue to develop in order to stay ahead of electronic systems.

The consciousness is the most obvious direction for the development of those biological systems – with us, human beings, taking the lead. For the time being, it's easier for man to build a skyscraper than it is to penetrate his own consciousness. People feel more at home in front of the TV than in the world of their own experience. No matter how you look at it, more than three-quarters of human life is spent in unconscious activity. Despite the talents with which we explore space, most of the time we just do whatever comes to mind, with all the expected consequences: conflicts, poverty, hunger, war, loneliness, heartbreak...

But history offers us hope. Evolution is marked by breaks in trends. Problems always lead to new solutions. Once – millions of years ago – oxygen was a poisonous gas that was produced by the first bacterial life on Earth. It became concentrated in the atmosphere and threatened to suffocate that tender life below. You might call it the first gigantic environmental crisis. Salvation came through the development of organisms that took in that same oxygen, started "breathing" – organisms that lived on oxygen. There are more examples. When hunting and gathering became unwieldy for the growing population, agriculture was born. The harvesting of fields made it possible for people to settle in one place. The industrialization of the last century was another answer to the social constriction of the feudal agrarian society organized around small villages with a great deal of social control. Industry brought with it the free life of the city. The Industrial Revolution brought human rights, democracy and even the welfare state, but since then material progress has run aground in social alienation. On the other hand, the consumer society is now suffocating in worldwide pollution. In other words, industrialization creates more problems than it solves. It's hard to imagine that Star Trek – that is, *more* technology and communication – is really able to offer solutions to these serious problems.

It's more likely that Albert Einstein once again has the right answer: problems cannot be solved at the same level at which they were created. Like the bacteria that transformed themselves into breathing organisms, life must keep growing towards new levels in order to survive. A deepening of the consciousness might prove to be a solution for humanity's current problems.

Perhaps environmental pollution, overpopulation and the contrast between rich and poor do not constitute the major problems of our world. Perhaps the answer to those challenges lies in the attitude people adopt when they encounter the world – that is, in human consciousness.

For Freud, man was determined by elementary, material passions – the need for food, sex and security. Matter does indeed provide security, but more matter does not provide more security. And more money does not make us happier. The serious problems of modern civilization can be attributed to the fact that advancing material development has not gone hand in hand with spiritual development. External evolution demands internal evolution. That was the element that Abraham Maslow added to "defensive" Freudian needs: man's search is for meaning, significance. He strives to develop his consciousness, to achieve self-fulfillment.

Spiritual development as a goal for humanity is not a new idea, of course. It's a theme that's been around for six thousand years. Enlightened spirits such as Lao Tse, Confucius, the writers of the Indian Upanishads and Rig Veda, Buddha, Socrates, Plato, Moses,

Christ and Mohammed all devoted their lives to this pursuit. But they were lone voices in their day. The information age has put consciousness at a more prominent place on the human agenda than ever before. An ever-growing communication web is linking billions of individuals together. People influence and inspire each other with increasing speed and frequency. And this means that insights find their way with greater ease. In other words, Jesus didn't have CNN at his disposal.

Another consequence of the development of the world brain is that abuses are immediately unmasked. Kosovo and Indonesia arouse the public consciousness and stimulate social change and renewal. The wave of mergers in the business world provides the same impulse, oddly enough. Research shows that three-quarters of the problems confronting organizations are caused by poor communication. Mergers challenge people to communicate better, listen better, understand better. In this way, global economic development – the perfect example of the material – undergoes growth of consciousness as well.

The fascinating experiments by the British biochemist Rupert Sheldrake suggest that there are many more possibilities for communication than we now realize. Sheldrake has shown that if a rat in a particular laboratory learns how to make his way through a maze, other rats in a quite distant laboratory quickly develop the same skill. And what about the dog that always lies on the doormat when his master comes home – even if that master, for the sake of the experiment, keeps coming home at unexpected moments. Sheldrake has also shown that telepathy between people is more than coincidental, and he is convinced that we can consciously develop these talents. In other words, they can expand their consciousness.

For thousands of years, the human spirit has been held prisoner by the patriarchal struggle to conquer and dominate. In her book *The Chalice and the Blade*, Riane Eisler writes: "Our minds have been stunted and our hearts have been numbed. And yet our stri-ving for truth, beauty and justice has never been extinguished. As we break out of these fetters, as our minds, hearts and hands are freed, so also will be our creative imagination." Self-direction is the logical next step in human development. Self-direction is the new name for freedom. People will be more and more involved in designing their own lives. For centuries, external direction has been the model. There were rules that had to be followed, and examinations and police were the means for compelling obedience. That "totalitarian" system has shaped the conditions for the following evolutionary phase. You have to build the roads first before you can drive on them. In other words, the discovery of possibilities precedes the selection of possibilities. The time has come for the spirit to escape from the institutes, organizations, structures and systems. The current development of the economy, technology and society is bringing human autonomy closer and closer. The modern individual has much more of a chance to organize his own life, far more than previous generations. Man is standing at the threshold of a "revenge of the spirit." This is the top of Maslow's pyramid: self-fulfillment. It is consciousness that separates the human being from other living creatures. Each person is recognizably unique and individual, and his desire is to fulfill that uniqueness. That could be the next evolutionary phase: growth towards becoming a conscious creature who directs himself.

If growth of consciousness is the mark of the future, this will have a profound effect on the way we equip and organize our world. When we think of globalization today, we only think of the economy, of matter. The challenge is to come up with a proposal for spiritual globalization and its effects on human beings and society. In this way, people will find themselves on the spiritual path to realizing that every individual, every creature, is part of a greater whole. As economic growth encourages competition, so spiritual growth encourages cooperation and a sense of connection. Individual spiritual development on a large scale – in contrast with the collective, mass-hysteria of the various religions – adds a new dimension to evolution. This does not mean that paradise has been attained. It means that the world will start looking different – less emphasis on domination and power, more space for self-organization. Less winning or losing, and more spontaneous synergy on the road to a common result. More self-direction in education and health care, fewer standardized lessons and standardized care. More technology, but more human communication, too – telepathy, for instance. Undoubtedly robots will be part of our future, but why should be make a mobile phone call in the future if we can read each others' thoughts?

Growth of consciousness could change the world profoundly. This is a perspective that is difficult to imagine from our current world view. Peasants living in the agrarian society of a few hundred years ago could hardly have imagined that one day everyone would be able to read and write. Yet that is the norm in the industrial age. In the same way, "consciousness literacy" will be a universal feature of the future. The flood of spiritual reading matter in the book shops and the rapidly growing number of workshops and courses are signs of things to come. All those readers and students are searching for more in their lives than material prosperity, although for many it's all no more than cautious exploration. That development is also an indication of what our own contribution might be. We can give ourselves the time and space to listen more carefully to what is happening within. We can actively focus on those projects and initiatives that we recognize as early precursors, that we recognize as the possibilities of the future. Those developments are the stuff that the future is made of. People have always created the things that they first imagined. We might regard the first photos of Earth taken from the Moon as birth photos of a new evolutionary phase, the birth of a deepening of the consciousness. On his way back to Earth, astronaut Edgar Mitchell was overcome by a sense of universal connection. A blue ball with its own organs and arteries, an unmistakable unity that transcends the differences plaguing our lives. Mitchell said, "The presence of divinity became almost palpable and I knew that life in the universe was not just an accident based on random processes."

Maybe you don't have to travel through space to realize this. Maybe the French summer nights are enough. In the end, what an Indian master once told me is what really counts: "the greatest journey we can make is the journey within." That journey begins with feeling, listening, looking and experiencing, and sometimes by taking a moment in our busy lives to invite the future in, to discover that happiness is more than matter of property, to learn that health is, first and foremost, an individual, inner experience. Those who begin that journey will not only change their own lives but will be contributing to a different, more human world.

I do not believe in the inevitability of progress. I only believe in change.
 – Gerald Taylor

EPILOGUE: BECAUSE PEOPLE MATTER

This book arose out of a cover story from Ode. We wanted to know how the economy was able to seize power, why practically everything today is dominated by growth, profit, bigger and more, why money does matter and people usually don't. That search led to the simple insight that the current state of the world economy is not a consequence of an accidental convergence of circumstances but is the direct result of human choices and decision. The rules did not make us; we made the rules – and that means we can make new, different decisions to achieve different results. There's no reason why we cannot come up with a number of fundamental changes in the current – inhuman – economic rules and thereby bend the process of globalization in the direction of a world economy in which people matter. A new method of calculating the gross national product that takes people and nature into account would help society kick the habit of economic growth. The adoption of the interest system was perhaps one of the most unfortunate choices our forefathers made, and the adoption of interest-free currency would clearly demonstrate that society can function better, and more harmoniously, if money is not linked to interest. Canceling debts would be a recurring obligation for creditors; it is a precondition for justice. The basis of trade would be exchange – reciprocity – and that is quite different from the worldwide export war being waged today. Taxes would help direct the economy. Taxing work is inhuman. Taxing consumption would protect nature. And a tax on international capital transactions would raise a great deal of money for development in the Third World. Finally, changes in the partnership law would restrain the stampeding influence of multinational corporations.

It's a militant agenda, but you can hardly call yourself a radical revolutionary if your goal is to help people, *all* people, get ahead – at the expense of big money and its power. It's also an agenda that could easily lead to despair. It's hard to imagine the colossal interests that dominate the world today making way for new ideas. We're always inclined to think that continuing on the chosen path is unavoidable, that globalization and Americanization are irreversible processes. But continuing on the chosen path is not inevitable. Change is inevitable.

I've often tried to imagine what it must have been like to dream of a free world from some garret in Prague or Moscow; how difficult it must have been to cherish that belief while "inevitable" reality was right outside, down in the street; how extra difficult it was because you could only discuss your dreams with your friends in a very cautious whisper. But a great deal of whispering did go on. Finally the whispers were spoken aloud and written down, and that power was enough to cause a concrete wall to collapse. *That* was inevitable. It's also inevitable that the gross inequality and injustice in today's world will be set aright. There will not always be a few people getting shamelessly rich at the cost of millions of poor. There will not always be such constant growth in the differences between North and South, as well as among the inhabitants of the rich countries of the world. Stock markets will not always play this game of chance, a game that has nothing to do with ordinary life. We will not always look on this spectacle with such a lack of concern, hoping to get our piece of the pie.

This is more than a garret dream. Remember that general voting rights did not exist a hundred years ago. Remember that someone split a church in two by nailing a document on a door.

Remember that somber prophets of the nineteenth century predicted the existence of massive piles of horse shit in the streets of the cities. Remember that once – millions of years ago – oxygen was a poisonous gas that threatened to suffocate life on Earth, and that humanity owes its life to the organisms that were transformed and began absorbing that same oxygen. The question is not whether change will come, but when. And we are in a position to influence that answer. We can do more than whisper, because ideas are free in our world – another achievement, by the way, that owes its existence to change. The ideas that have been brought together in this book are already growing. There are much thicker, more detailed books devoted to the same ideas. There are web sites, demonstrations and conferences.

Fortunately, there's more than one path leading to change. New ideas are emerging simultaneously in a variety of forms, merging together and multiplying. Changes take time, but the reform of the world economy has already begun. It's up to human individuals to demonstrate leadership and get the process going, to produce a new reality for tomorrow. This is not an overestimation of our abilities. Human beings are not all-powerful and all-decisive. But every person can say and do what he thinks is best in his life. That influence counts, and it is decisive. Naturally, we should always keep in mind Gandhi's warning of "dreaming of systems so perfect that no one will need to be good." The change is not only a matter of outer rules but of one's inner mentality as well. It will take more than a few new agreements to put the brakes on greed. But doing your inner homework does not release you from the moral duty to raise your voice when you see injustice being done. And who doesn't see that? Who chooses to remain blind?

Each person's answer demands a combination of courage, patience and hope.

The courage to say that the emperor has no clothes, when everyone else refuses to see it. The courage to say, with vulnerability and authenticity, that which no one else dares to say.

The patience to overcome frustration, disappointment and resistance. The patience of the garret in Prague, to hold fast to the ideal when reality is most intransigent.

And hope. Hope is not naïve, but functional. We need hope to find the strength to realize new possibilities, to solve problems and penetrate dilemmas. We need hope to create a different future.

Because people matter.

RESOURCES

Introduction
Arundhati Roy, "The Greater Common Good," Outlook, *1999.*

Chapter 1.
Richard Douthwaite, The Growth Illusion, *Green Books, 1999.*
Jonathan Rowe & Judith Silverstein, "The GDP Myth," The Washington Monthly, *March 1999.*
Bill McKibben, Hope, Human and Wild, *Little Brown, 1995.*

Chapter 2.
Bernard Lietaer, The Future of Money, *Random House, 2000.*

Chapter 3.
Michael Rowbotham, *The Grip of Death, A study of modern money, debt slavery and destructive economics,* Jon Carpenter, 1998.
Ann Pettifor, "IMF and World Bank – Soviet style Banks," *The Guardian,* September 19, 2000.
Will Hutton, "Debt-relief campaign Jubilee 2000 can now claim its great victory, thanks to Leviticus," *The Observer,* October 3, 1999.
Revista, *Renancr Indiavista,* issue 7.

Chapter 4.
Paul Hawken, "N30," www.natcap.org/sitepages/art73.php.
Colin Hines, *Localization, A Global Manifesto,* Earthscan, 2000.
Lori Wallach and Michelle Sforza, *Whose Trade Organisation?* Public Citizen, 1999.
Michael Rowbotham, *The Grip of Death, A study of modern money, debt slavery and destructive economics,* Jon Carpenter, 1998.

Chapter 5.
Geoff Mulgan, *Life after Politics,* Fontana Press, 1997.
Alvin & Heidi Toffler, "21st Century Democracy," *New Perspectives Quarterly,* Fall, 1992.
Eckart Wintzen, "Een duurzame vrije markt," *Ode,* January/February, 1996.
Howard M. Wachtel, "Trois taxes globales pour maîtriser la spéculation," *Le Monde diplomatique,* October 1998.
Heinz Stecher, "Time for a Tobin Tax?" Oxfam GB, May, 1999

Chapter 6.
Paul Hawken, *The Ecology of Commerce*, HarperBusiness, 1993.
Kalle Lasn, *Culture Jam, The uncooling of America*, William Morrow, 1999.
David Harris, *The Last Stand, The war between Wall Street en main street over California's ancient redwoods*, Random House, 1995.

Chapter 7.
Ivan Illich, *Medical Nemesis*, Random House, 1976.
Lynne McTaggart, *What Doctors Don't Tell You*, Thorsons, 1996.
Andrew Weil, *Spontaneous Healing*, Alfred A. Knopf, 1995.
John Robbins, *Reclaiming Our Health*, H.J. Kramer, 1996.
Walter A. Brown, "The Best Medicine," *Psychology Today*, September/October 1997.
New Scientist, March 30, 1996.
The Ecologist, November/December 1996.
World Watch, November/December 1996.
The Organic Farming Sourcebook, The Other India Press, 1996.
Christopher Flavin & Nicolas Lenssen, *Power Surge*, Norton, 1994.
Hermann Scheer, *Sonnen Strategie*, R.Piper & Co., 1993.
Eurec Agency, *The Future for Renewable Energy*, James & James, 1996.

Chapter 8.
Jurriaan Kamp, "Je werk of je leven," *Ode*, September/October 1999.

Chapter 9.
Arnold Cornelis, *De logica van het gevoel*, Stichting Essence, 1997.
Peter Russell, *The White Hole in Time*, Aquarian Thorsons, 1992.
Deepak Chopra, *Ageless Body, Timeless Mind*, Harmony, 1993.
Riane Eissler, *The Chalice and the Blade*, HarperCollins, 1987.
Jon Spayde, "The New Renaissance," in, *Utne Reader*, January/February, 1998.
Roger Walsh (ed.), *Paths Beyond Ego*, Tarcher Putnam, 1993.
Duane Elgin, *Global Consciousness Change*, www.awakeningearth.org

Epilogue
E.F. Schumacher, *Small is Beautiful*, Blond & Briggs, 1963.
Bill McKibben, "The End of Growth," *Mother Jones*, November/December 1999.

DO YOU LIKE THIS BOOK?
We have good news.

This book started as an article in *Ode*, the monthly international news magazine, based in the Netherlands – and you can get a free issue.

Ode focuses on provoking ideas, inspiring initiatives and – most of all – on people who care to change the world. *Ode* is the bridge between the conventional and the new thinking, between the economy and the environment, between the North and the South.

Beginning in January 2003, *Ode* is being published in English for worldwide distribution.

Get your free issue at **www.odemagazine.com** or contact us by phone: +31 10 4360 995.

THIS BOOK IS A PARAVIEW SPECIAL EDITION

The imprint Paraview Special Editions focuses predominantly on publishing select out-of-print titles. Thanks to digital print-on-demand technology, it is easy and efficient to bring out-of-print titles back to life again, in essence making valuable books available to new audiences. Paraview Special Editions will also focus on publishing works of international authors and co-publishing projects with like-minded partner organizations, such as associations, magazines, and non-profit organizations.

For more information about Paraview Special Editions, visit our website at www.paraview.com

WANT TO KNOW MORE ABOUT PARAVIEW BOOKS?

A complete list of our books and ordering information are available at www.paraview.com. Paraview titles are immediately available on amazon.com, barnesandnoble.com, and other online bookstores, or you can order them through your local bookseller.

Leadership in a New Era
Edited by John Renesch
$16.95/£12.99

This collection of vision and wisdom for tomorrow's business leaders is presented by a group of outstanding men and women in a joint collaboration. This rare combination of business executives, professional consultants, successful authors, and leadership scholars has come together with a common theme: new times call for new leadership. Their collective voice calls for a fundamental transformation in the way we lead, the way we see leaders, the way we allow ourselves to be led, and how we think about leadership.

Competitive Business, Caring Business
Daryl S. Paulson, Ph.D.
$14.95/£12.50
This book is designed to provide managers and executives with new tools and methods for finding personal satisfaction in their unique contributions to the teams, companies, or industries they serve. Daryl Paulson, the CEO of BioScience Laboratories, Inc., has successfully combined science and business in his personal and professional life and demonstrated in clear, simple, practical terms the true meaning of "integral business." He shows how the work of Ken Wilber, the world's foremost human science theorist, applies in the business domain, and explains why the process of "doing business" must be considered in a holistic and integral manner if it is to meet the needs of the 21st century.

PARAVIEW PRESS and **PARAVIEW SPECIAL EDITIONS** use digital print-on-demand technology (POD), a revolution in publishing that makes it possible to produce books without the massive printing, shipping and warehousing costs that traditional publishers incur. In this ecologically friendly printing method, books are stored as digital files and printed one copy at a time, as demand requires. Now high-quality paperback books can reach you, the reader, faster than ever before. We believe that POD publishing empowers authors and readers alike. Free from the financial limitations of traditional publishing, we specialize in topics for niche audiences such as mind/body/spirit, science, business, and balanced lifestyles. For more information, please visit our website at www.paraview.com, where you can also sign up for Conscious Planet, Paraview's free monthly media guide.

9 781931 044455

Printed in March 2021
by Rotomail Italia S.p.A., Vignate (MI) - Italy